DATE DUE

FEB 1 3 1991 BIRD	FEB 25 '91	
MAR 2 5 1996	FEB 2 6 1996	

Demco, Inc. 38-293

The Dream That Was No More a Dream

A Search for Aesthetic Reality in Germany, 1890–1945

Bill Kinser · Neil Kleinman

Coordinated by Lynn Musgrave

"You ought to have known how to create a fantasy for yourselves, not to act it for me, or anyone coming to see me; but naturally, simply, day by day, before nobody, feeling yourselves alive in the history of the eleventh century . . . waking up in the morning, getting out of bed, and entering straightway into the dream, clothing yourself in the dream that would be no more a dream, because you would have lived it, felt it all alive in you. You would have drunk it in with the air you breathed; yet knowing all the time that it was a dream, so you could better enjoy the privilege afforded you of having to do nothing else but live this dream, this far off and yet actual dream! And to think that at a distance of eight centuries from this remote age of ours, so colored and so sepulchral, the men of the twentieth century are torturing themselves in ceaseless anxiety to know how their fates and fortunes will work out! Whereas you are already in history with me . . . And sad as is my lot, hideous as some of the events are, bitter the struggles and troublous the time—still all history! All history that cannot change, understand? All fixed forever! And you could have admired at your ease how every effect followed obediently its cause with perfect logic, how every event took place precisely and coherently in each minute particular! The pleasure, and the pleasure of history, in fact, which is so great, was yours."

Luigi Pirandello,"Henry IV"

Schenkman Publishing Company, Inc.
Cambridge, Massachusetts

Contents

Acknowledgments

Originally this book was planned as a monograph to be published by the Depot Press of Urbana, Illinois. Thanks to it and its parent organization, The Depot, Inc., which is an experimental center for the performing and creative arts, we were encouraged to begin thinking about this project.

The manuscript was read and criticized at various stages by Richard Wasson and Harold Walsh, and also by Heinz and Mai Von Foerster, who lent us some of the visual material we used. We value their pointed criticisms and their patient probing.

Faith Baron Frost, Christine Frey and Michael Hays aided us with the translation of the German text that appears in the notes.

Cynthia Merman of Harper and Row labored to acquire permission to reprint quoted and visual material. And we are indebted to Ann Close, also of Harper and Row, who provided coherence when we needed it most.

Nathaniel Billingsley rendered design and editorial assistance.

Das Symbol des Reichsparteitages der Ehre

As the title and subtitle of this book suggest, we approach Germany—often a vague and diffuse entity even for Germans themselves—as though it had a continuous consciousness. Our intention is not to personalize Germany and its history, nor to invent a German *Zeitgeist*—an invisible and amorphous spirit that loosely justifies all. We believe that societies produce parallel and interconnected systems of expression and statement which reflect a total social complex of meaning and value.

With varying degrees of enthusiasm, societies try to articulate the logic of these interconnections through their use of myth and historical interpretation. Yet these explanations come from *within* a society; therefore, they are part of the total complex of meaning, not above or outside it. Hence such explanations by a society of itself add but another level to the total complex of meaning, without being able to take in the significance of what they have added, for they cannot study their own reflections. The way in which a society explains itself—the style and purpose of its history—is, therefore, as important as the specific content of its history.

Some societies are particularly interested in explaining themselves to themselves and in producing a social system and history that will validate these explanations. Germany is a classic example of one of these societies. For that reason, we treat the German consciousness as though it belonged to an artist, one who has deliberately constructed a pattern of historical meaning and events so that the beginning must imply the end. Throughout this book, we discuss why this was true for Germany and what this means.

We have said that the structures within a society reflect and present the values and meaning of the entire system, that is, each component part of a society has a homologous relationship to every other one as well as to the whole. Another way of saying this is that each social feature, or level—for example, the political institutions developed to carry the society forward, the pattern of social life, the very buildings erected to house social and political activity, the style and shape of social myths and the configurations of historical action—each one of these carries the stamp of the total social enterprise.

It is important to be clear on what is implied by this approach: ours is an aesthetic analysis of social systems. We can find the assumptions of this kind of analysis most sharply defined in their more traditional setting, that of literature. André Maurois in his study of Charles Dickens provides us with a good example of the aesthetic frame of mind:

> What is a novel? Very simply, a narrative of fictitious happenings. Why do we need such narratives? Because our real life is passed in an incoherent universe. We long for a world subject to the laws of the spirit, an ordered world; through our senses we know only obscure forces, and beings with confused passions. From the novel we seek a universe which will help us, wherein we can seek emotions without exposing ourselves to the consequences of authentic emotions; find intelligible characters, and a Destiny on a human scale. To fulfill this role, then, it would seem that a novel should contain two elements: on the one hand, an image of life, a story in which we can believe, at least so long as we are reading it, failing which our reading would be wearisome and we should return to ourselves; and on the other hand, an intellectual construction, grouping these natural images according to a human order.*

In this passage are the basic articles of faith of almost any literary critic: art is an intellectual construction subject to laws of order; art through its form makes coherent a confused and obscure reality; and finally this form presents a credible image of life. From this reliance upon the inherent form of art, all else flows; the critic extrapolates his critical methods and his evaluations about good and bad art. A case in point: the literary technique which assumes that one may take one paragraph from a novel, examine its style and form and the relationship of style to content in the passage at hand, and then may elaborate, from this analysis, the logic, vision and meaning of the entire novel. If the passage being studied contradicts, for no purpose, the logic of other passages or the logic of the entire novel, the work is taken to be faulted—perhaps importantly so. In the universe of aesthetic forms, then, it is assumed that the part reflects the whole, or should. As we have said already, each level has a homologous relationship to every other level as well as to the whole.**

For readers of structural anthropology, this aesthetic doctrine will sound familiar. To quote Claude Lévi-Strauss:

> No science today can consider the structure with which it has to deal as being no more than a haphazard arrangement. That arrangement alone is structured which meets two conditions: that it be a system, ruled by an internal cohesiveness; and that this cohesiveness, inaccessible to observation in an isolated system, be revealed in the study of transformations, through which the similar properties in apparently different systems are brought to light. As Goethe wrote:

> *All forms are similar and none are the same,*
> *So that their chorus points the way to a hidden law.*

> This convergence of scientific perspectives is very comforting for the semiological sciences in which social anthropology is included. Signs and symbols can only function in so far as they belong to systems, regulated by internal laws of implication and exclusion, and the property of a system of signs is to be transformable, in other words, *translatable*, in the language of another system with the aid of permutations.†

The structuralists, then, take the logic of aesthetic theory one step further than that indicated by Maurois, although this step was always implied: society is itself an intellectual construction, subject to the laws of order; through its form, it makes coherent a confused and obscure reality; and social forms, like art, contain a set of metaphysical values and meanings (or the way in which the society relates to and perceives reality) which is discoverable.

What the aesthetic and structuralist approaches suggest is that we may refine the various levels of society—

---

* André Maurois, *Dickens*, trans. Hamish Miles (New York: Harper & Brothers, 1935), pp. 121–22. Reprinted by permission of The Bodley Head, London.

** Cf. Erich Auerbach, *Mimesis*, trans. Willard Traske (Garden City, N.Y.: Doubleday, 1957), for a brilliant application of this method.

† *The Scope of Anthropology*, trans. Sherry O. and Robert A. Paul (London: Jonathan Cape, 1967), p. 31. Published in the United States by Grossman Publishers, Inc.; reprinted by permission of Jonathan Cape.

levels that on the surface appear quite different and unconnected—and after extracting the essential pattern of each, we should find comparative logics and meanings. We have tried to make comparisons of this kind throughout the book. We examined, simultaneously, certain patterns in German history (for example, Bismarck's wars of consolidation, the World War I Schlieffen plan and Hitler's blitzkrieg) and certain patterns in popular art (e.g., the use of the feudal myth); after studying each we compared them to see if they were translatable into each other and, therefore, shared a commonality of perception and meaning.

We discovered not only that a translation between German history and art was possible but that the Nazis had deliberately intensified the feedback between the two. This feedback was, it turned out, the basis for their propaganda; it allowed them to aestheticize reality and historicize myth. But we also found that this impulse to aestheticize reality was itself a basic element in the meaning of German history, even before the emergence of Hitlerian propaganda.

Maurois offers a hint as to what this aesthetic impulse may mean when he says that we need narrative fictions "because our real life is passed in an incoherent universe. We long for a world subject to the laws of the spirit, an ordered world. . . . From the novel we seek a universe which will help us, wherein we can seek emotions without exposing ourselves to the consequences of authentic emotions. . . ." This, too, was the purpose of the aesthetic in Germany. It became clear to us that the Germans needed an aesthetic reality because they felt they lived in a totally incoherent universe, a universe in which they were uncertain about their national identity and, thus, uncertain about their individual public identities. In short, they felt vulnerable. This vulnerability is expressed in German history (the mixture of fascination with and fear of a second front woven into the battle plans mentioned above) and was also expressed in popular art (the continual images of a feudal kingdom). What linked the history and the art was this common expression of vulnerability—what we have called "the myth of the feudal kingdom under siege." And what was characteristic of this expression in all its permutations and elaborations was—as Maurois says—an attempt to "seek emotions without exposing [oneself] to the consequences of authentic emotions. . . ." In this, one finds the essential meaning and nature of German propaganda.

We have said that, to find out whether one level of German society could be translated into another, it is necessary to refine the levels of German society. This is a process of reduction and simplification that attempts to condense the variety and diversity of the social mixture until the nonessentials have been left behind, leaving only the fundamental elements in their purest form. The task, then, is to discover the equation that will link them together. Since this process of reduction, simplification and condensation is also the method of German propaganda (a method which became the content of Hitler's Aryan doctrine), and since the purpose of the totalitarian system was equally to translate one level of society into another (in this case to make individuals interchangeable), it seems important from the beginning to understand what this process entails.

We may call the equation that links social or cultural elements together a cultural metaphor, for it functions in the same way a literary metaphor does: one starts with the perception of dissimilarity and then attempts to discover a yoke which will creatively bond these dissimilarities together. In such a definition of metaphor, we stay within the limits set by Aristotle's observation that metaphor is "the perception of the similarity of dissimilars."* We must also remember that a metaphor is not necessarily static; it is susceptible to permutations. But no matter how much the surface of a metaphor seems to change, its basic elements remain constant. What is more, the relationship among its elements remains fixed. (Thus one may write: $A + B = C$ or $A = C - B$ or $B = C - A$ or even $C = A + B$.) Each formulation has a different emphasis, suggests a different priority, but the values remain the same. Hence, although the specific point of balance or outer configuration of a metaphor may change, the basic distance and tension of the elements cannot change. Applied to a study of culture, this means that an important clue to the meaning of a culture is to be found not only in the basic metaphor—its basic elements—but also in the shift in balance and in emphasis between the elements of that metaphor.

This clue suggests an interesting problem. The elements a society is attempting to balance turn out to be surprisingly limited in number. A satisfactory balance does not seem impossible to develop, the permutations are many but not infinite; yet the balance between these elements is never quite achieved—except perhaps in primitive societies. First one side of the equation and then the other has too much weight, too disproportionate an emphasis. We begin to notice that the elements that are so precariously balanced are often the culture's most bothersome "dissimilars," its most crucial concerns. A perpetual imbalance built into a cultural metaphor raises an important question: Is the imbalance itself critical to the meaning and purpose of the metaphor? (The nature of Germany's metaphor seems to indicate that the answer is yes, although Germany's effort to construct a viable cultural metaphor was motivated by the conscious wish to do away with this imbalance.)

The implications of this question can at least be partially answered by returning to Aristotle's definition of metaphor. His view assumes that the fact of dissimilarity always remains even after the metaphor has been made, for it is only in the marriage of dissimilars and the resulting tension caused by this marriage that the making of metaphor has value. Therefore, if the metaphor were totally successful in achieving a permanent unity, thus absolutely destroying the ability to perceive disparity, it would also destroy its reason for being. With this reading, Aristotle's definition becomes a description of the nature and structure of thought, especially post-Aristotelian thought: the mind does not wish to create a finished unity, although it appears to be striving after it; it reaches instead for perceptions that counterfeit unity. The very virtue of cultural metaphors lies in their ability to counterfeit unity while at the same time being able to take advantage of the dynamism of built-in imbalance.

When we pick up German history in 1890 with the removal of Bismarck from power, we soon perceive that under Bismarck the German metaphor had become frozen and therefore useless. It is in the peculiar nature of cultural metaphors like Germany's—informed as it was by the vision of vulnerability—that successful stabilization of dissimilars threatens their societies more than imbalance. A culture's reason for being is imperiled. The problem with Bismarck's solution was that he had too

* *Poetics* XXII.

completely managed to control the dissimilarities; he provided a classic fatigue that was not sufficient. The result was a unity so total that it seemed to be counterfeit. It lacked luster; it had lost its inherent tension. Hence Bismarck's unity seemed merely spurious and empty.

Germany under Wilhelm II moved back toward the logic of vulnerability and imbalance. And because it did, it could also renew its search for unity. As we shall see, Germany's concept of unity affected both the style of its history and the facts of its historical existence. The attempt to make unity led to Germany's manifestly artificial and theatrical political style. And paradoxically, the concern for unity brought Germany to the disunity and dislocations of World War I. It appears that Germany could afford unity—and then lushly and extravagantly—only when the dynamics of imbalance were in motion; that is to say, when unity did not threaten stability. (We do not discuss Hitler here—although obviously he would fit in quite nicely—because we will consider his experiments with the unity of artificial forms in some detail later in the book. But we should say in passing that Hitler and Goebbels as well as the Nazi propaganda machine were the first to recognize that propaganda must provide order and instability at the same time, if it was to be successful.)

Thus far, we have simply tried to sketch out the general manner in which the aesthetic method approaches a social system. But it may be worthwhile to stand back for a moment in order to collect any of the assumptions and implications of our method that may remain hidden. First, we assume that reality (or, quite loosely, the flux of events in the past and present) is to be perceived and understood in the way we understand any art form. Thus we look for its symmetries and asymmetries, its leitmotivs or archetypes, its world view or vision and its metaphors and their variations.

But how do we begin to find these patterns? We start with a set of ground rules: we may exclude one detail in favor of another, since there could be no meaning if we were surrounded by an array of details, each of which had equal claim upon our attention. Hence we begin to select. We try to recognize those details that have similarities or that are in some way identical, and then we try to organize them. We sift out the "relevant" details from the "irrelevant" and subordinate one fact to another. Finally we put together a structure in which the parts do not contradict the whole, in which the logic is consistent, in which the obscure has been given meaning because it is informed by order. All this time we have worked with the belief that if we could remain objective and consistent and honest about what we saw, we would discover a truth inherent in the details that we have been sorting through. Have we discovered truth? Perhaps, but certainly a truth. Still we must wonder, did we discover this truth or did we create it? If the man at work is an artist, one says he has created a truth—but with artists, one does not quibble over words. On the other hand, if he is a historian we insist that he has made a discovery— or else he must be a charlatan.

We must stick with this mock argument because it takes us very near a serious question that has been hovering behind our discussion. "What is a novel? Very simply, a narrative of fictitious happenings." If we accept the historian as a creator, an artist, it seems that we shall have to say that history too is "a narrative of fictitious happenings" and that reality is also fictitious.

There is, however, another route through this maze, the one taken by Henry James. When faced with this question in the course of discussing the art of fiction, he said "the novel is history." He then went on to say that the view that holds the novel is "making believe," or is composed of fictitious happenings, is a view which "implies the novelist is less occupied in looking for the truth (the truth, of course I mean, that he assumes, the premises that we must grant him, whatever they may be) than the historian. . . . To represent and illustrate the past, the actions of men, is the task of either writer. . . ."* Henry James solves the problem, then, by making art a vehicle for truth, a truth no less true than that of the historian. Reality—at least what we can know of it— appears safe; it is not to be relegated to the realm of fictitious happenings.

Nevertheless upon reconsidering James's statement —"the truth, of course I mean, that [the artist] assumes, the premises that we must grant him, whatever they may be . . ."—we find that we are back where we started, with the question of objectivity; but we now find that our concept of reality has been drastically altered. If we must grant the artist his premises, whatever they may be, we have given to the artist, and the historian, an immense power over reality. Henry James, not surprisingly, knew this. In a letter to H. G. Wells, he writes: "It is art that makes life, makes interest, makes importance, for our consideration and application of these things, and I know of no substitute whatever for the force and beauty of its process. . . ."** And by "art" James means "form." Form has force and beauty! With that, we find the realm of aesthetics considerably enlarged to include not only history but also all systems of meaning, all constructs that depend upon order for their existence and value—hence even political ones, or for that matter logical ones.

Perhaps we go too far. But we do so intentionally. For, as we started by saying, we treat the German consciousness as belonging to a deliberate artist. We have, in part, already explained what we mean by this: that Germany can be analyzed in the way one analyzes a work of art. What we shall try to show in the course of this book is a more intriguing dimension to this problem—one that we have indicated was true in the case of Nazi propaganda: that the German consciousness treated its own reality—developed and lived its history—as though it were a work of art. It was a culture committed to its aesthetic imagination. And through this commitment, it extended and exaggerated the principles of the aesthetic beyond their original, self-contained universe: they became political statements, serving to prescribe as well as to describe. By Hitler's time aesthetic principles had become precepts like the following: life is form (or order); force is beauty; and force is meaning.

Obviously the effect of the aesthetic perception upon the perceiver is to reorient the perceiver's relationship to reality. Reality takes on a sensuous richness, for it, too, is now a work of art; all around him shines with new clarity. Still he is an observer, detached much in the way of a visitor in a museum. A logical (but not necessary) next step is for the aesthetic imagination to turn upon itself—upon the observer, thus making him into a work of art. But even when the observer sees himself a participant, he still retains his air of detachment. (This

* "Art of Fiction," *The Portable Henry James*, ed. Morton Zabel (New York: Viking Press, 1965), pp. 394–95. Reprinted by permission of Charles Scribner's Sons.
** *Ibid.*, p. 489; James's italics.

double perspective is not unlike that created for the audiences of modern dramas or reserved for characters within these dramas.)

To be both participant and observer—engaged and detached at the same time—changes the shape of reality. Reality is transformed into a drama in which the actors are permitted a heightened awareness of their own value and identity. In such consciously perceived drama, everything is pregnant with significance, full of connections and implications; every event becomes "a moment of truth" and every decision, an act of definition.

Pushed too far, the ability (or desire) to perceive reality aesthetically—as was the case in Germany—can be disastrous. It can lead to a distortion of the real, producing the grotesque and the surreal. It leads to the "reality" of propaganda where truth and identity become subject to the "force and beauty" of form; a kind of visual hypnosis results. But despite these dangers, the ability to perceive reality aesthetically is still essential to our ability to understand the meaning of reality and, in turn, to understand history. We must be able to stop the process and flux of reality—freeze it, stand back from it and ourselves—if we are to see the long-term implications of present decisions and events as well as to make some sense of the past.

Nevertheless, whatever the necessities (and virtues) of aesthetic imagination, there are obvious risks in using a methodology based upon aesthetic principles. The reader cannot help but be aware of the fact that our critical theory reinforces the very applications of aesthetic perception we intend to examine and to criticize. Such an overlapping of method and subject may seem a curious (or worse, futile) exercise. Yet such an exercise can, perhaps, be instructive, if only to make apparent the limits and implications of the critical language we are speaking.

To the degree that an aesthetic system reflects its own limits, it has parted company with the aesthetic system that makes possible propaganda and social manipulation. For as we shall see, propaganda deliberately tries to silence the internal, verbal and discursive dialogue we carry on with ourselves. We lose much without this discursive dialogue; we become victims in dramas we act in but cannot understand. If we can create a reflexive aesthetic, we are freed from the totalitarian threat that the aesthetic implies. We are, at once, aware of the methods by which form produces meaning and, at the same time, reminded that certain forms create and, thus, structure reality for us.

The basic theory of aesthetics and symbolic drama used in this book owes a great deal to the theories of four men: Kenneth Burke, George Herbert Mead, Jurgen Ruesch and Jacques Ellul. Burke focused the attention of a whole generation of critics upon the meaning of dramatic form. While working in primarily literary and aesthetic terms, he made apparent a larger strategy: that an understanding of the metaphor of theater had applications beyond what is normally considered the domain of the aesthetic; that what we know about theater might be interchangeable with what we can know about reality; thus, that the method one uses to analyze drama might be used to analyze social and political forms as well. A consequence of Burke's thought was that one was enabled *to see the social process within space*, as a framed arena in which the behavior is according to the principles of drama.

Mead came at the issues from different angles, those of sociology and psychology, although his conclusions and techniques were strikingly similar to Burke's. He contended that social groups are structured social dramas with the members of the groups gaining identity through symbolic roles and relationships rather than through any necessary identity or meaning they as individuals bring to the groups. In the theories of both Burke and Mead, the "character" or "identity" of a man is subordinate to the form or context (or drama) in which he exists.

Ruesch's contribution was to locate and codify the grammar of objects, those designs, costumes, settings and décor—in short the visual and dramatic material of a culture—that constitute a nonverbal language. Finally, Ellul outlined the meaning and methods of sociological propaganda, explaining how action can create belief (what he called "orthopraxy"). Perhaps Ellul's major insight was exactly this: that belief need not produce action, but that action—almost inevitably—produces belief in the actors.

A Word on the Organization of This Book

We start with the history and end with the pictures; but, since they are equivalent and related sections, the matter could have been easily reversed. In between the historical discussion (Chapter I) and the pictures (Section Two), we try to show why and how we connect history to pictures. Chapter II develops a theory of symbolic and aesthetic forms out of a discussion of the models we found in German history and through a consideration of the explanations Germans gave for their history. Toward the end of this chapter, we analyze the way in which both Hitler and Goebbels manipulated the aesthetic and symbolic dramas to create propaganda. Chapter III is given over rather completely to an analysis of the pictures presented in this book. There we try to make explicit the exact configuration of the German symbolic drama. To introduce this chapter, we show the link between nonverbal language and symbolic dramas; to end it, we explain how and what we looked for in the pictures. In Chapter IV we stand back to gain a wider view of some of the issues raised earlier. Our interest here is with the aesthetic principles of propaganda and the propagandistic power of the aesthetic. Leni Riefenstahl's documentary-propaganda film, *Triumph of the Will*, is looked at in some detail. In the very last portion of this chapter, we re-examine Germany's historical fascination with its boundaries, frames and borders from a strictly aesthetic point of view.

Section One   An Essay

I   The History: Conflicts and Confusions

The removal of Bismarck from the office of German chancellor, in 1890, by Kaiser Wilhelm II provides for us a convenient wedge into the grain of German history. Bismarck had been the central German political figure for twenty years and more, starting his career under Wilhelm I (Wilhelm II's grandfather) before the German nation had come into existence; he was, in fact, the architect of Germany's nationhood. And then suddenly, only two years after a very young Wilhelm II found himself unexpectedly on the throne, Bismarck was gone. It seemed as if something in full flight had vanished without reason.

Yet, by 1890, Bismarck had already become inappropriate to the new spirit of Germany—a spirit, as we shall see, he had been responsible for releasing. Hence Wilhelm II took no political chances when he removed Bismarck. The times demanded something new, even if the German people could not quite say what it was. So they paid lip service to the legend of Bismarck, even after he had left the scene, but they no longer found passion or meaning in his political words and perceptions. A new style was needed: a man who had become everyone's grandfather was to be replaced by a dandy who was everyone's king. Age was displaced by youth—not in itself a remarkable occurrence, but the German nation itself seemed, in the ascension to power of Wilhelm, to pass from the style of a crafty adulthood, as represented by Bismarck, to the style of an action-oriented childhood. In reading German history, one senses that with the removal of Bismarck the nation became younger as it grew older.

However dramatic the dismissal of Bismarck seems to be on the surface, we shall later argue that there is much in the thought of the grandfather that prepared for the actions of the dandy. But before trying to relate the one to the other, it is important that one should have some sense of the pressures at work in Germany which made this radical change in political style so necessary.

If there is anything one can say about Bismarck's political virtue—a virtue that had carried him and Germany successfully through twenty years—it was his ability to accommodate opposites. And opposites and contradictions Germany had in profusion. Germany had developed an economic system that was both industrial and feudal. In addition, it had developed the beginnings of a social structure that was, on one hand, middle-class and corporate while, on the other, hierarchical and paternal. It is easy to see why Germany could support these extremes for as long as it did: middle-class corporatism is in many ways like a feudal hierarchy, both being versions of a contractual arrangement that precisely spells out the order of society and the social rewards to come, if this order is maintained. But it should be equally clear that a growing industrial system must eventually eat away the premises of a feudal order; the industrial creates a middle and working class with social and political needs for mobility, which a feudal system cannot satisfy.

Conflicting assumptions also existed in Germany's identity as a nation. It was a model that depended for its meaning upon a mixed set of definitions and points of view: nationalism as the feudal kingdoms saw it, nationalism as the liberals understood it, nationalism as the Prussian imperialist used it and nationalism as the middle-class economy desired it.

Bismarck's feat was to make an operating model out of these conflicts, to make a "Germany" where no German had previously existed. But he was not a detached political scientist, impartially developing a master plan. He brought to the definition of Germany his own commitments: he worked in the name of the Prussian Kaiser Wilhelm I; thus, his motive was to establish a Prussian empire, an empire that would satisfy the long-standing Prussian desire for expansion within the German-speaking community to the well-established boundaries of Austria-Hungary.

But because Bismarck recognized the variety of reasons others had for the creation of a German state, he was quite willing to have his Prussian empire called a German nation and willing to let others define "nation" in the ways that would disturb them least.

For the individual feudal kingdoms absorbed into his new system, a German "confederation" seemed a logical solution to their military and economic vulnerability; they saw it as a model for survival in the new Europe forming around them. To diminish their uneasiness over even the idea of confederation with Prussia, Bismarck worked on them through their military and economic weaknesses, persuading them to accept alliances that met these needs. Once this was accomplished, he was later able to transform these alliances into more binding political agreements. That the feudal kingdoms ultimately discovered they had lost their autonomy was partly due to the fact that Bismarck was, at the same time, responsive to other levels of the German imagination: the German people —that is, the subjects of the individual feudal states— wanted a nation.

Bismarck's Germany was taking shape in a historical period when the thought of liberals had merged with the economic needs of the bourgeoisie. The issue of nationalism was important to the liberals, sufficiently important that it swept many parts of Europe (including some parts of Germany) into revolution in the late 1840s and early 1850s. The mood of the German middle class was not, in general, revolutionary, but it did need the economic foundation and psychological stability that a nation could provide, and it, too, identified with the sentiments of nationalism.

One of the important steps in Germany's actual progress toward nationhood, which puts in perspective its confusion over the meaning it gave to nationhood, was a necessary disengagement from the suzerainty of the Austro-Hungarian Empire. Because of the necessity of the separation, most Germans came to feel that "Germany" must be in some way a repudiation of all that Austria-Hungary stood for—that is, the politics of the *ancien régime*, Metternichian conservatism and internationalism. The liberals were pleased by this turn of events: they found Germany on a course that seemed to lead away from the conservatism they had opposed. They had been handed a political victory of sorts and had reason to expect that in the new Germany there would be a political opening for them. Yet in spite of Germany's apparent commitments to, and investments in, liberalism and the middle class and its opposition to internationalism, it had for its central pillars of value the expansionist vision and the conservative-aristocratic sensibilities of the Prussian state.

At another level, we may observe these contradictions as they were mirrored in the structure of individual German classes. Each group denied time and again its avowed beliefs and its basic self-interest. Thus the Junkers moved against their interests by underwriting the process of industrialization and expansion; for, in the long run, both of these destroyed not only Junker political authority but also Junker agrarian and feudal traditions. (Bismarck perceived the dangers of expansionism to the political structure he was committed to; as we shall see, his expansionism was severely restricted. Unlike most Junkers, Bismarck did not treat expansionism as though it were an end in itself. When we turn to a comparison of Bismarck and Wilhelm II, we shall be able to see more clearly the nature of this conflict.)

If the Junker class misunderstood its best interests, the same was true for the other classes within German society. The middle class, which had a great deal to gain by remaining faithful to its liberal and civilian origins, provided—often at exactly the wrong political moments—the very political support required to assure Germany's continued authoritarian and feudal structure. Hence it defeated itself by depriving itself of an opportunity to acquire the power and weight it yearned for. The same self-betrayal was true for the working class. Frequently it discarded its list of grievances in order to come to the aid of its political and social opponents—always in the name of nationalism—at the very moments that national confusion placed its goals within reach.

One may well observe that these kinds of self-defeating contradictions appear in many countries, and especially in those countries that developed national identities in the latter half of the nineteenth century. In fact, Germany's specific problems—industrialization versus an older agrarian tradition, and a middle class tempted by national conservatism while simultaneously demanding a liberalization of both political and social institutions—appear to be problems shared by most nineteenth-century nations.

What distinguishes Germany from most of the other nations of this period is that Germany was faced by the complete spectrum of these problems within the short span of a generation. It had tried to move from an essentially medieval, feudal and fragmented culture into an industrialized and nationalized society in one stride.

Germany was also different from some other countries in having commenced this enormous social upheaval without the internal release of a major revolution. The German middle class became established in relative social peace; at the same time, a working class more committed to the issues of nationhood than to questions of its class identity was produced. But Germany's price for its peaceful transition turned out to be a growing vagueness in the national dialogue, noticeable restlessness and alienation among its citizens, and a general confusion over identity and social roles.

To diminish this uneasiness, Germany underwent a subtle shift in focus after Bismarck's dismissal. To do this, it did not reassess its contradictions so as to come to terms with them or root out those that could not be resolved. It did quite the opposite; it tried to paper them over. Therefore instead of continuing to perceive and accommodate contradictions as Bismarck had done, Germany, with Bismarck gone, now hoped to synthesize a new whole, making a social unity out of its polarities—but polarities it no longer cared to understand. To achieve this synthesis, it was quite willing to simplify its history and the meaning of that history as long as such simplification promised a suitable set of consistent social roles for its citizens.

Before turning, however, to the specifics of Germany's solution after 1890—especially as they were embodied in Wilhelm II's foreign policy and his political style and vision—let us return to Bismarck's strategy of accommodation in order to see how it worked and what it entailed.

Bismarck's genius had been to balance and juggle the contradictory forces—exactly those central to Germany's malaise. He neither resolved nor simplified them, nor did he wish to. His political style was based upon the principle of controlled imbalance: he perceived contradictions and conflicts and then used them. Through this ability to recognize the ambiguities and shifting motives of groups or individuals, Bismarck derived a shrewd flexibility; he was free to maneuver around his opponents, throwing them off balance or manipulating them. And this flexibility worked equally well against both his foreign enemies and his domestic opponents. For this reason Bismarck's handling of Germany is illuminating because it puts in the sharpest light the jungle of contradictions that become more buried, and therefore less accessible for analysis, in post-Bismarckian Germany.

To handle the question of the liberal reform impulse within his authoritarian concept of nationalism, Bismarck emphasized consolidation over reform. In his presentation of consolidation, Germany was envisioned as potentially a mighty fortress. This notion had special appeal to most Germans (even the liberals), since the constant threat and reality of invasion during their divided past gave the issue of defenselessness a nightmare presence. In his struggle to keep the appeal of consolidation alive, Bismarck enforced domestic policies like the Kulturkampf, "a campaign for cultural freedom" that promised to purge the German fortress of "un-German" ideologies. More important in his project, however, was his use of foreign policy. His decisions in this area were made as much to present the German people with the specter of invasion as to forestall the fact of real invasions. At times this meant that he had to manufacture threats, or discover them—something he was quite ready to do. As his success and events proved, he gauged the potency of the nightmare fear correctly; pressure for social reforms almost always collapsed under his tactics.

Bismarck's ability to link the promise of consolidation with threats to German security satisfied simultaneously two distinctly contradictory impulses: expansionism and isolationism. As a Prussian and a Junker, Bismarck had always seen the enlarging of Prussia as necessary for Prussian security. To this end, he had for the most part persuaded the rest of Germany that the expansion of Prussia was subordinate to German nationalism. In his preliminary steps to form a "German" empire (the wars against Denmark in 1864, against Austria-Hungary in 1866 and against France in 1870—all basically Prussian wars), he managed with virtually total success to make the wars appear "German." What is interesting is that Bismarck was able to maintain his fiction even after he presented the Reich constitution of 1871, which made it perfectly clear that essential control of Germany was to rest permanently with the Prussian Kaiser and his minister. Even Bismarck's battle slogan of "blood and iron" served a double purpose; it echoed the Junker military spirit while sanctifying and nationalizing its expansionist tendency. In short, two things had actually happened under Bismarck: Prussia had expanded and Germany had been formed.

Yet, in spite of Bismarck's expansionist fervor, the long-term effect of many of his policies pointed Germany in a quite different direction—toward isolationism. Although it may seem somewhat strained to call Bismarck an isolationist, especially if one recalls his nearly continual involvement in (and actual intrusion into) the affairs of Europe, his foreign maneuvering did have an unequivocally isolationist design. It was to separate Germany from Europe, to isolate it, to free it from the possibility of invasion; but most important, it was to make Germany impervious to what he viewed as dangerous economic and political instability in surrounding nineteenth-century Europe. Evidence of his isolationism can be found in much of his diplomacy: his protectionist tariffs, his disinclination for colonial adventure and his labyrinth of treaties that prevented alliances against Germany and kept Germany from commitments that might trip it into war. And through all this, by artfully using the threat of war, he justified military expenditures, thereby preserving Germany's military and diplomatic credibility, and—with the same effort—preserving his political credibility with the Junkers.

Bismarck's policies taken together reveal a national model that is centripetal and corporate. Its cohesion and strength came from being pushed inward from outside. Its purpose was to develop an economically and diplomatically self-contained and self-sustained system. It was to be an amalgam of the older feudal pattern and the newer industrial goals. Germany's political gravity depended upon a balanced set of opposing forces. Bismarck accommodated opposites in order to preserve the equilibrium of a socially static, nationalist center while he simultaneously took advantage of the technological revolution.

But what must also be recognized in Bismarck's handling of Germany is that his political style, in spite of its inherent rigidity, gave the national system the appearance of fluidity. Bismarck affected this by rarely moving absolutely in any one direction; he seldom formed a political coalition or signed a treaty without having at hand other options. His intention was not to foreclose the future, and its effect was to keep a number of possibilities hovering on the political horizon at any one time. He felt it important to keep the future open, for he understood that the future is always subject to reversals, some valuable, others regrettable but unavoidable. This perception generally served him well, except during the last few years of his career when either his instinct finally deserted him or his sleight of hand simply became too transparent to be effective against the build-up of social and political contradictions. In any case, by the end of his tenure he had been allied at one time or another with virtually every political party in Germany, including groups he had previously persecuted and tried to destroy.

The result of Bismarck's foreign policy was twenty years of peace. But this peace worked to disrupt the stability of Germany that Bismarck had labored for. It created, instead, a chain reaction that made peace itself untenable. First the effect of peace, together with Bismarck's domestic policy, marked a development of Germany's industry and an increase in its productivity. And, of course, because of this industrial expansion, new economic and political classes grew. But the Prussian in Bismarck could not give these classes the kind of substantive power that would have recognized them, legitimized them and allowed them a coherent voice in the government. Still he had given them, regardless of his intentions, sustenance. Peace had, if nothing else, provided them with the occasion for prosperity and the needed stability to take advantage of it.

Ironically this "stability" was to be the undoing of Bismarck's own vision of stability. The middle class was fortified, the expectations of the working class were expanded, and the appetite of the industrialists was whetted. Their demands grew increasingly insistent; they needed satisfactory political roles. Peace also had a disquieting effect upon those in power, the very class Bismarck identified himself with. The Junkers—the only group with a recognized and established tradition of political authority—were left with no wars to fight. Their military stance was on the verge of hollowness—full of the parades and barrack maneuvering of a peacetime army. In addition, their hereditary leadership seemed to them endangered by the rising influence of the industrialists. Underoccupied and threatened, these Prussian Junkers felt a growing frustration and restlessness that was edged with hostility. In short, no group had a well-defined sense of purpose that could be successfully reinforced and clarified through action.

Given this situation, by the late 1880s even Bismarck's historical image was turned to his disadvantage. The clarity of his early doctrine of "blood and iron" indicted his later quite skillful diplomacy. Judged in the light of his earlier martial postures, his diplomacy looked pale and aged, if not corrupt. Thus, Bismarck's early career cast a shadow that blotted out the meaning of his long-term vision. The romance of Prussian expansion and German consolidation, the legends of Bismarck's own victories in the 1860s, remained, waiting to be retranslated into the dream of colonies and a pan-Germany; and these dreams violated Bismarck's fundamental principle: Germany would not survive if it could not avoid war in Europe. Thus Bismarck, his policies and their logic had created a social and political blur; the more effective they were, the more they reinforced the contradictions and ambiguities of individual Germans. Since the policies could not provide a unified and consistent style, they only helped to exaggerate and exacerbate the strain and confusion of rapid change.

After Bismarck, Germany quickly moved toward a series of extreme positions that only served to limit its options and diminish its flexibility. With near-abandon, or so it seemed, Germany closed out options in the future, tying itself instead to courses of action which made the future inevitable. The effect was exactly opposite to that of Bismarck's strategy, which, it may be remembered, had been to avoid the inevitable by keeping open future alternatives.

After 1890, Germany's new direction was most apparent in its foreign policy. By discontinuing the treaty with Russia, carefully maintained by Bismarck so as to avoid the threat of a two-front invasion, Germany exposed itself to exactly this eventuality. And once vulnerable on its eastern front, Germany was then forced to throw its lot in with Austria-Hungary. This too, Bismarck had warned against. He saw Austria-Hungary as an intrigue-ridden and dying bureaucracy, far too corrupt and irresponsible to build a mutual-defense alliance upon. Yet now, as a result of its new policies, Germany had inextricably linked itself to this moribund empire's irrational diplomacy and whims. Finally, in order to embark on colonial adventures, Germany greatly expanded its navy; and both of these decisions meant confrontation ultimately with other sea and colonial powers, especially England. The events leading to the First World War proved the truth of Bismarck's warnings. In every instance Germany had selected the alternatives that made war inevitable.

Germany's growing urge after 1890 to transform the optional and contingent into the inevitable and necessary bespeaks a powerful underlying frustration with complexities, the ambiguous and the irreconcilable. The intricacies of Bismarckian accommodation had finally taken their toll. The fragments and disparities to be balanced had multiplied beyond the point where they could be held together, and Bismarck's delicate, centripetal equilibrium collapsed. The path taken by Wilhelm II to reconstitute the society—namely, simplification—could not, of course, solve its problems. The process of industrialization still continued and still threatened to destroy the feudal hierarchy completely. But the directness of simplicity gave the illusion that Wilhelm's policy was indeed a program that would work.

Wilhelm II, upon displacing Bismarck, refeudalized the empire by incorporating the civilian and middle classes into roles originally reserved for the Junker aristocracy. He did not do this deliberately—he was too much an absolutist and Junker himself to wish to dilute the aristocratic role—but the end result of many of his policies was, in any case, to make available the feudal ideal to those not originally part of it. It is important not to underestimate the consequence of this: the German middle class (and by indirection, the working class) at a critical moment in its development found the roles of the hierarchical, aristocratic establishment opened to it. The traditional collision between middle-class aims and the feudal structure that had seemed all but a certainty in Germany was prevented for the time being. The burgher's son and the landowner's son could, instead of competing with each other for power, identify equally with the forms of nobility.

Wilhelm II's colonial policies provided domains and power for the sons of influential mercantile-trader families. His reorganization and expansion of the navy into a German service, rather than a Prussian one, allowed the middle class to enter the military tradition, receive posts and adopt styles that had previously been inaccessible to them. His ennobling of important industrialists made participation in the aristocracy attainable, the climb up the hierarchy possible.

But Wilhelm's most important achievement in the period after Bismarck's dismissal was his ability to absorb into his role the image of authority that had been vested in the early career of the Chancellor. He merged the sacredness of the throne and the destiny of Germany with the historical authority and authenticity of Bismarck's political and military victories. Wilhelm II stood with a history behind him; his dynasty, Germany, was already established. It was this history, which had already softened into myth (a process he helped to extend and elaborate upon whenever he could), that he offered the German people.

Wilhelm had several qualities that especially recommended him for the role he was to play at the moment in German history he was required to play it. He was young, and must have appeared particularly young when his twenty-nine years of age were compared to Bismarck's seventy-three. He was fascinated by the flamboyance of the military, proudly parading in a variety of uniforms in public and private and insisting that all German officers do the same. He was an impatient man, little interested in theory and not at all intrigued by subtlety or nuance;

he liked the bold and admired the man of action—a type he fancied himself to be. His extemporary speeches were reported as masterful, as having a glib grace and fluidity. He enjoyed the public, delighted in performance and used the throne as a prop and Germany as a stage. All in all, he was a distinct contrast to the old Bismarck.

Still, despite Wilhelm's flurry of activity, his style, his youth and his policies, he eased Germany's cultural confusion only temporarily. His version of the feudal kingdom was only an instinctive act of simplification made possible by his temperament and his unequivocal view of himself in his role as kaiser and emperor. His vision of Germany did not encompass all the realities of the lives of other Germans. And no matter how bold and brave his style, the German people facing him had to see in their current kaiser a maker of policy. Therefore, at the same time that they could be liberated by his dramas, they were reminded, because he was a real political figure, of their connection to an immediate German history with consequences.

It was this connection of history to consequence that Germans since Bismarck had, in fact, unconsciously hoped to sever: their historical reality presented too many alternatives, too many ambiguities, too much confusion over purpose and values and too heavy a burden of anxiety for decisions made. Wilhelm, because of his own political and historical reality, could never quite escape the burden of history, nor could he provide a successful avenue of escape for Germany.

All the same, Wilhelm is significant. While he could not provide an escape from historical realities, he could help in recasting the shape and meaning of the past by making it seem mythic instead of historical: he could make available to the popular imagination the romantic conception of the feudal kingdom. By this refeudalizing of industrial Germany, Wilhelm was able to offer middle- and working-class Germans a mythic past and glory they, as a group, had no historical claims to. Through such an investiture, they were presented with the opportunity to mythicize their present and transform their class reality.

Wilhelm had given the majority of Germans a chance to cease their muddled flirtation with the liberalism of bourgeois thought and middle-class goals. Many Germans, in some sense, did. After 1890, the realities of Germany remained, of course, the same. But the nation increasingly turned its attention to the mythic past for its understanding of the present, rather than using its historically informed present to prepare for the future. Industrial Germany was on its way to doing what no other industrial state had managed to do: to remain a feudal kingdom.

II Myth and Symbol: History Fulfills Itself

The mythic, like any statement, organizes meaning by highlighting and shaping details and by arranging them into a declarative plot. A myth explains the past, the present and the future, and its narrative shape establishes its historical reliability—or at least that is its purpose. But declarative or narrative form does not make every myth a truth, any more than it makes any other kind of statement true. In some cases, the mythic may be pure distortion, an invention whose purpose is to falsify the meaning of the past. Nevertheless some myths are fair interpretations of the past and recognitions of basic patterns (archetypal patterns) that appeared and will reappear when specific circumstances are present. There is a problem, then, in distinguishing a mythic invention from the legitimate recognition of an archetypal pattern. This difficulty is most particularly apparent in the case of Germany as it attempted to retain in some form its feudal identity.

Bismarck's model of Germany, for instance, was in some measure a solution to a real historical problem, a problem that Germany had faced in its feudal form and one that had been central in persuading the feudal kingdoms that a unified Germany was in their best interests. Before its unification, Germany had indeed been the victim of countless invading armies; therefore it had a long memory of encirclement, siege and vulnerability. In quite reasonable response to this memory, Bismarck had constructed his centripetal, corporate system, erected his protective tariff walls and developed his subtle isolationist diplomacy. His wish had been to create a walled fortress which would be able to withstand siege if attack could not be avoided, and which would be able to satisfy its internal needs while the siege lasted. He envisioned a Germany that was self-contained and self-sufficient.

When the confusions of German society weakened Bismarck's system, Wilhelm's response to the memory of former invasions was simply to reverse the centripetal direction of the German state. This produced an expansionist, centrifugal state that still retained the old grammar of vulnerability, encirclement and siege. But now, in place of preventive diplomacy and a self-contained economy, Wilhelm and his ministers lowered tariff walls, planning to replace them with the walls of empire. The new colonies were to extend the enclosure, so as to include within it a new source of raw materials and a new market for finished goods. And instead of preventive diplomacy, Wilhelm and his ministers talked of preventive wars as the solution to the threat of invasion.

In comparing these two political models, we can see that the dissimilarities belie their fundamental unity. Germany *was*, after all, vulnerable. It was surrounded by powerful and established nations who had been tempted by the ease with which German fragments could be scooped up, and Germany's history of invasions showed that this temptation was often indulged. While both of these models tried to offer political and economic solutions to this long-standing German problem, the solutions they offered—rather ironically—only perpetuated and sometimes accelerated the crisis of vulnerability. Bismarck's unification of Germany and his establishment of an empire—whatever his intentions—pushed Germany right into the circle of the powerful and now suspicious neighbors it had been trying to avoid: France, Russia and Austria-Hungary. Wilhelm's expansionist policies inexorably led to the confrontations of the First World War. One might add—to continue this progression of self-induced vulnerabilities—that Hitler's strategies produced not the thousand-year Reich but the very sort of disaster he (and Germany) had tried to escape.

Germany's long-term history suggested an archetype, the recurring image of which the Germans were quick to recognize. The perpetual German dread, the glance over the shoulder at the enemy who may be about to attack, has its most distinctive formulation in Wagner's *Ring*

cycle, in which the infamous "stab in the back" is administered to heroic Siegfried by a dwarfish and clearly alien Hagen. The theme is picked up by Hitler in *Mein Kampf* in his explanation of the German defeat of 1918, where once again, it seems, "the warring German Siegfried received a stealthy stab in the back."[*] This fear was written into the strategies of both the First World War Schlieffen plan and the Second World War blitzkrieg: in each, the central aim was to neutralize the western front with sufficient dispatch so that Germany could turn to protect its exposed rear. The hysteria of an enemy at its back, thus, lead to the fantasy of "three-week" fronts. When Germany raced west, it did so with a distracted, and distracting, foreboding of an enemy in the east.

In Germany, one discovers that a set of historical facts has developed into a mythic declaration with a prophetic power. The logic of such a process is simple and circular: Events and situations require explanation. Explanations—universalized, generalized and given imaginative flesh—become myths. Myths shape perception. Perceptions produce policies. Policies cause events and situations. And (to begin again at the beginning) events and situations require explanation. How *can* one separate the beginning of the circle from the end, the mythic invention from the archetypal situation, or the fabrication from the candid recognition of a geopolitical fact? They share a self-perpetuating cycle. The first feeds the last, and the last vindicates—and reinstates—the first. This cycle is what Freud meant by "the self-fulfilling prophecy" —the manufactured statement that creates historical circumstances, thereby validating itself.

For Germany, the original, historical vulnerability of the divided states called for a larger, more protective nation-state. But once established for this reason, it continually returned to situations that would justify its existence by reconfirming its vulnerability. Solutions seem to demand the old problems, else what is the value of the solution? Hence, Germany's need to confirm its national meaning made vulnerability an essential part of its continuing myth, for it was the original pattern of vulnerability that informed Germany's concept of "nationhood." To subtract vulnerability from the equation would have demanded an entirely new definition of the term "nation." Of course, this process of national confirmation through weakness cut across the major purpose of the myth's rhetoric, which was to give to the nation a vision of heroism, energy and success. On one hand, the myth presented the role of hero; on the other, it required the condition of victim. Some way had to be found to join these contradictions.

It was necessary to produce minds or perceivers who would not perceive the contradictions. And to do this, it was necessary for Germany to break with the present, to make impossible a reading of the present that exposed the realities hidden there. Germany had to dwell in the past if it was to escape the meaning of the present; yet even this past had to be treated in a special way, or else it might signal truths Germany could not afford to hear. The past that Germany entered could have no present, because the present reminds one of the events of the past that have made this particular present what it is. (We have seen that this was Wilhelm's problem in his position of real political figure.) A recognition of the relationship between past and present would have made clear to

* Adolph Hitler, *Mein Kampf*, trans. John Chamberlain *et al.* (New York: Reynal & Hitchcock, 1939), p. 912, reprinted by permission of Harcourt, Brace & World; cf. Peter Viereck, *Meta-Politics: The Roots of the Nazi Mind* (New York: Putnam's, 1965), p. 139.

Germany the logic of its myth; and it was precisely this logic that Germany did not wish to understand: that to be a hero it had first to be vulnerable; that to fulfill its myth and desires it had first to be degraded and betrayed by them.

A number of attempts were made to portray the German myth. Each did in a way manage to enunciate its unique integrity without exposing the implications of its larger logic. And although each was only partial, each deepened the meaning and fascination Germany had for its slowly crystallizing mythic statement. Conservative social critics like Julius Langbehn and Moeller van den Bruck, for example, looked to the past for meaning, but they made the mistake of trying to use that past to explain the details of the present and, thus, returned to the present even as they tried to escape it. They catalogued evidence which seemed to them to prophesy the imminent collapse of Germany. Yet in direct contradiction to their sense of Germany's inevitable doom, they were able to prophesy that salvation and glory were somehow immanent in the facts of Germany's present. Fritz Stern in speaking of their work remarks, "It was as if their own Jeremiads on the real evils of the present so frightened them that they were forced to project a future or a regeneration beyond all historical possibility."*

Richard Wagner provided Germany a mythic reality of another sort, a reality that totally excluded the present. Through the elaborations of his operatic plots as well as through the experience of seeing them performed in the hermetic and florid environment of Beyruth, Wagner gave his audiences an opportunity to escape from present time in an artificial cycle of fixed history. He was the artist of Germany's dream. Yet despite this total Wagnerian environment, his audience did finally have to leave the theater. His theatrical reality could only be suggestive, a moment free from history and outside the struggle and confusion. The proscenium was still there. Beyond Beyruth was still the historical Germany.

Hitler's contribution to the process we have been considering was to take Beyruth's aesthetic drama and make it into an explicit, national drama. He is different from Bismarck and Wilhelm II in that the content of their myths was always just below the surface—an implicit symbolic drama. Hitler treated the myths openly, as if they were self-evident truths. And he is different from writers like Langbehn, Moeller and Wagner in that he would satisfactorily (or persuasively) translate aesthetic roles into the public reality.

In Hitler's favor was the fact that when he emerged, Germany was in a state of extreme and real crisis. Its defeat in the First World War, the resulting breakdown of the social structure and the economic collapse had wiped away virtually all possibility of perpetuating earlier social roles. The unsatisfactory identities that had been maintained by tradition and habit were destroyed with the destruction of the social and economic order. Poverty and chaos are in that way great levelers; few identities or roles remained which could pull individuals back into a historical past. At the same time, the prophesied doom had come. By the time Hitler came to power, the German search for unambivalent social roles had become an absolute necessity. The historical present and the mythic past had for a moment converged (one might think that Germany, in fact, had unconsciously made them converge).

Hitler believed in the power of the aesthetic but took the aesthetic one step further than Langbehn, Moeller or Wagner; he believed reality could be treated like any theatrical form—susceptible to fabrication and manipulation. And he not only believed in the ability to fabricate but in the power of fabrications to be real. ("The Greatness of a lie always contains an element of being believed."*) Thus he was able to stage ceremonies, know the details of their construction, and yet still be pleased and surprised by the organized ovations and cued adulations. He was not caught in a self-awareness that forced him to see that his reality was his own fabrication. He had become a propagandist of self—one who could create a dramatic role and identify without remembering how it had been done—and it was this model he presented to the Germans and to Germany.

Mein Kampf was his experiment with himself. In it he created a biographical, or past, self. At the same time *Mein Kampf* projected a living self—the Hitler who lived concurrently with the audience that read the biography. The function of this living self was to fulfill the prophetic voice of the biography; in turn, the function of the biography was to establish the authenticity of this living Hitler. Hitler's experiment was to merge the historical tense and the present tense in order to move beyond the historic into the mythic.

The relationship of the *Mein Kampf* Hitler to the living Hitler is similar to the relationship of the Old Testament Messiah to the New Testament Christ; one vindicates the other. Like other "religious" scripture, *Mein Kampf* is an attempt to merge documentable history with undocumentable myth, an attempt which makes myth documentable and present history mythic. When the documentation becomes—as it did in the case of Hitler—the underpinning of myth, the net effect is that reality can become a self-contained event. It is no longer related to, or changed by, the passing of time. And it is this timelessness, an escape into the mythic, that Hitler gave to Germany.

He made programmatic the various versions of the feudal myth that had existed before him and constructed the drama with a simplicity that made obvious and self-evident the roles to be played. Every defeat, every failure, was a justification and a vindication. The history of defeat was redeemed, by itself becoming a myth that was being fulfilled in each moment of the present. The feudal kingdom was encircled and under siege, would, in fact, always be under siege. This continuous threat of a potentially tragic end hidden in every moment made every role significant and every defeat promising.

With Hitler's success at fabricating and projecting a myth, Germany concluded the undertaking begun by Wilhelm II. On one level, Germany had settled finally on the content of its social drama; it now had a clearly visualizable set of roles and diagram of actions. But equally important is the style this drama took. It was increasingly characterized by high melodrama and accentuated theatrics, especially apparent during the Hitlerian period, when the German myth was articulated through a series of mass-rally performances.

Germany's theatrical style grew directly out of its confusions and its search for identity. Such theatricality is, in fact, one of the chief symptoms of a society undergoing an identity crisis. This is natural enough, for soci-

---

* *The Politics of Cultural Despair* (Berkeley, Cal.: University of California Press, 1961), p. 269. Reprinted by permission of The Regents of the University of California.

* Compare Arthur Koestler's short essay on this sentence, entitled "The Great Crank," in *The Yogi and the Commissar and Other Essays* (New York: Macmillan, 1967).

eties in attempting to define themselves become extremely self-conscious. Their dialogue is cluttered with discussions of "national purpose" and "national heritage and tradition"; they scrutinize their "culture," consider whether they have one and what it might be. While to some degree salutary, such public soul-searching can be debilitating because it intensifies the very crisis being explored. Social self-consciousness imposes a proscenium on the society as well as the citizens. And in the case of the individual citizen, he feels as if he were "on stage," plagued by a numbing sensation that he is only an "actor," but uneasy because he has a role still to discover.

Societies have deliberately taken advantage of this need for roles, especially in times of crisis, when the weakness of identities is most obvious. They construct new social identities not only to stabilize the individuals within their community but also to limit the number of roles available. This limitation is most important to societies in stress, since it makes social regulation and control easier. They are helped in this control by the citizens themselves. Once an individual has found an acceptable role, the general confusion and his private ambivalence tempt him to be no more than the role requires. For this reason, even though a national scenario may be coercive and repressive (as it ultimately was in Germany), it appeals to individuals because it guarantees coherence and form. In this cycle, we witness a self-regulating system, one in which the weakness of social and political identity brings on a crisis and the crisis manufactures new identities, albeit simplified ones. Generally, in fact, it is this extreme simplification of the social drama that we associate with totalitarian societies: they are unitary and one-dimensional dramas in which everyone is asked, and most agree, to play the same part.

While it is true that such simplified social dramas can be caused and maintained by an intensified self-consciousness, it does not, of course, necessarily follow that all societies betraying self-consciousness are (or will become) totalitarian. The question at issue is how the society meets its self-consciousness and its need for drama. Nontotalitarian societies treat what we can call "theatrical uneasiness" as a symptom of cultural neurosis; they use it as a means to diagnose, locate and correct the neurosis and, thus, themselves. Totalitarian societies are encouraged—perhaps encourage themselves because their crisis is so paralyzing—to make a social virtue of the theatricality of self-consciousness; they program it into the system in such a way that the neurosis is institutionalized. What started as the symptom is now taken for the cure.

Germany is a good example of a society in which theatricality was institutionalized. We have already seen a portion of this process unfold in the theory of men like Langbehn, Moeller, Wagner and Hitler. The view of reality behind that theory together with that contained in the heightened sense of social drama we have just considered merged in Germany in a common proscenium—an aesthetic frame for reality that was imposed upon the normal political rhythms. The effect of a dramatic proscenium is to isolate men and institutions, then freeze them into rigid shapes, and finally to separate them from their normal backdrops. Individuals become artifacts, purposeful constructs that can be coaxed, controlled, manipulated and dismantled—treated in the same way raw material is treated by a craftsman.

In such an arena, a curious thing happens to the forms of reality: they become palpable. One sees them in three dimensions with rich and vivid substance. And as a result, one's sense of "meaning" and "truth" is altered. Truth, now based upon a version of optical experience, becomes equivalent to visual symmetry; and the mark of reality is an object's starkness. No longer following its normal continuum in reality, the object is "framed." Its viewer suddenly is aware of it as form, a self-contained dramatic event, and feels as though he is "seeing" it for the first time. The time within the frame is similar to that of theater. As with theater, the presentation is in present time—the ongoing time of the audience's normal world—but the performance engages the audience in a fixed pattern of time that can be played over and over again. This explains why the aesthetic is so perfectly suited to the institutionalization of a mythic past.

We have said that the imposition of aesthetic space upon social reality springs from a cultural self-consciousness, caused by the insufficiency of public and private roles. This is true, but such self-consciousness itself is rarely brought to a verbal or discursive level; frequently it remains submerged exactly because the process that brought these symptoms on is one which the society cannot afford to face. There is, after all, a difference, and a crucial difference, between being victimized by self-consciousness and being able to liberate oneself from it by understanding what it implies. However, even when the existence and oppressiveness of self-consciousness cannot be admitted, it (and the crisis that produced it) is expressed in a crypto-language—a symbolic code—that releases and works out the conflict without having to recognize its presence.

The symbolic is a drama in its own right, but not one its participants are conscious of being involved in; hence it is not the mythic statement a society articulates to explain itself. In fact, the symbolic drama determines social behavior without being the explicit or historically apparent cause for such behavior. If this is so, a symbolic reading of history requires a somewhat different relationship to historical facts and causes than is normal. For example, when individuals commit themselves to certain political acts or groups with a reasoned sense of what their commitment entails, one usually starts by assuming that their rationality has tried to take into account the political and social consequences of their decisions—they knew what they wanted and were acting to achieve it. Yet often a set of conscious decisions of this sort produce circumstances that are at odds with the original political intent. One may say at this point that the reason of the individuals acting was insufficient to understand the political realities. But when this happens consistently with an individual or a nation, one may choose to find instead another drama at work beneath the explicit surface, a drama which has nothing to do with "political realities." Thus, as we have tried to show, Wilhelm's actions mean one thing on a political level but imply an entirely different set of meanings beneath the literal surface. Wilhelm did not let the treaty with Russia lapse *in order to* make Germany vulnerable again; at least consciously, his intent was the exact opposite. For him the act made simple political sense. With the distance of historical vision, one can see that the act made no political sense but a great deal of symbolic sense.

We must stop here for definition. One cannot undertake a discussion of *the symbolic* without making certain distinctions, since the term, unfortunately, is muddied, having accumulated at least two meanings. The first denotes the visible agent that serves to reflect a hidden system of values, and the second stands for the hidden system of value itself. Thus the term *symbolic* expresses two quite different, although connected, levels of apprehension.

To make plain what these two meanings entail, suppose we imagine that reality can be simplified into a three-dimensional diagram, whose surface we can call our literal reality. Being on this surface, we can only guess as to the texture and composition of the internal material. But this substructure is important, for it not only supports but also molds the contours of the surface. So although we cannot get in immediate touch with this core, we still wish to find a way to get at least an indirect view of it. The literal reality is not useless; it does offer some help in determining what we wish to know. It is studded (at least we may imagine this is so) with jewel-like excrescences, bubbles that clarify the surface. And like prisms, they permit us to glimpse beneath the surface. What is confusing here is that the term *symbolic* can be applied equally well either to these prismatic agents or to the substructure. In the first case, a portion of literal reality (the prisms are, after all, on the surface) is designated as *the symbolic*. In the second case, *the symbolic* is only what can be seen indirectly.

By calling these prisms *symbols*, we are stressing their function to refer to the nonexplicit, their character as agents—that is, we stress their ability to "symbolize" meaning or, to use French structuralist vocabulary, to be "signifiers." In this sense, the Nazi swastika is symbolic; it is an explicit object that clearly represents a set of values. In the same way, the German Michael—the feudal knight figure in German art—is symbolic; it was for Germans a conscious representation of the myth they had adopted. According to this definition, a symbol reverberates with obvious significance. In fact, it is this ability to be so obvious in its prismatic function that makes it symbolic.

When we call the substructure symbolic, we are stressing what is referred to: what is implicit rather than explicit or, again to use structuralist vocabulary, what is being "signified." The difference between these two meanings is the difference between stating that the figure of the knight Michael symbolizes Germany's conscious use of the feudal myth and stating that this figure with its peculiarly German configuration *signifies* a part of a cultural drama—that part in which Germany, unconsciously attempting to divest itself of history, tried to give itself a childlike identity. (We shall discuss this identity in some detail in Chapter III.)

It is perhaps already evident that in this book the primary meaning of symbolic is this latter one—the unconscious cultural drama. Thus Germany's symbolic drama is not its explicit statement of the feudal myth, although the explicit may run parallel in form with the symbolic. Instead, the symbolic is the underlying structure of attitudes and desires signified by the particularly German implementation of the myth.

Symbolic drama of this type permits little or no detachment. One participates in it by being within the act, the word or the gesture—in short, by being *within* the drama. Consequently, it operates at the level of pure presence, pure act, pure word. And by not allowing consciousness, it is able to exist prior to the awareness of structure, even prior to its actual embodiment in structure. The identity it provides is the identity that *adheres* to the participant as he fulfills the *inherent* intention of his language or action. On this view, the symbolic is a rather silent force which nevertheless has a singular power to affect *who* one is.

The symbolic is a gentle and subliminal persuader. Its nature seems to place it in a direct conflict with the hard-edged awareness of the aesthetic. But this need not be the case; the aesthetic may, in fact, be but one more extension of the symbolic drama. We can return to an earlier discussion of the aesthetic to make this point clear. It has been observed that the aesthetic effectively sealed Germany off from the consequences of its history. If we are correct in contending that a part of the content of Germany's symbolic drama was the creation of a childlike identity free from the restrictions of guilt, time and experience, the aesthetic in satisfying this impulse also satisfies the symbolic. The same relationship between the symbolic and the aesthetic can be found in the aesthetic's ability to make neurotic self-consciousness into an acceptable private and public style. When serving to make the neurotic acceptable, the aesthetic serves the primary function of the symbolic, which is to create an integrated set of identities. To put it perhaps too baldly, one may read back through the aesthetic—even an aesthetic which denies the unconscious by emphasizing the self-conscious or which denies permanent identities by projecting a world of make-believe—and find on the other side the shapes of symbolic dramas and their meaning.

In a review of the propaganda of Hitler (and here one must include Goebbels), one can see how this subtle interplay between aesthetic and symbolic fitted the requirements of the Nazi totalitarian state. By first aestheticizing the symbolic drama (making the buried pattern of German culture explicit), Hitler produced perceivable forms which he had control over. He could tailor them to his needs. When he later made the proscenium inherent in the aesthetic almost invisible by making consciousness (or reflective thought) a crime against the state, he returned these forms to their subliminal condition—but now they had his stamp upon them. Because he was able to control the proscenium, he was also able to produce roles that settled the confusion over identity but destroyed the possibility of autonomous, private identities. In this way he substituted for self-conscious identities one-dimensional roles.

How did Hitler manage to collapse the proscenium and yet maintain control over the material in it? Goebbels' edict forbidding art criticism is a classic example of the principles of Nazi propaganda in operation: "The reporting of art will take the place of . . . art criticism. . . . The critic is to be superseded by the art editor. The reporting of art should not be concerned with values, but should confine itself to description. Such reporting should give the public a chance to make its own judgments, should stimulate it to form an opinion about artistic achievements through its own attitudes and feelings."* The effect and purpose of this edict *was not* (one must say this categorically even before discussion) to "stimulate" the formation of opinions; its purpose was the opposite, to stifle judgments. Neither was its purpose to liberate the audience from the tyranny of the critic. When it is dangerous to be a professional critic, it is equally dangerous to be a critical member of the audience. For both the critic and the audience, reportage became a general condition.

The principle underlying Goebbels' edict was to

---

* Quoted in George L. Mosse, ed., *Nazi Culture* (New York: Grosset & Dunlap, 1966), pp. 162–63.

denerve consciousness by neutralizing the act of seeing. The act of seeing was to become a stony gaze instead of remaining a way of perceiving—and conceiving. This meant that visual information was to pass through the eye in the form of sensory data, but it was no longer to be mediated by the mind. The eye (and the mind's eye) were to be transformed into simple glass windows, incapable of refraction. The net effect of this was to make the mind itself incapable of reflection. Seeing had, under Goebbels' edict, been changed into a pure act—an act no longer conscious of itself.

This condition stimulates not opinions but passive voyeurism; it creates not evaluators but passive observers. Under the kind of pressure suggested by Goebbels' edict, the intellect, no longer inclined to perform its analytical function, disappeared. And when it went, so went the capacity to absorb visual information while being aware that one is absorbing it. And so also went all the uniqueness of the mind that makes autonomous identity possible. The Germans were within the drama, unaware that there was a drama—neither able to assess it nor able to reject it. It simply was.

III   The Nonverbal and the Symbolic: We Are What We Observe and We Do What We See

Symbolic dramas are expressed in a number of ways. We have already considered some of them: the pattern of "real" historical events, the mythic statement that is formulated to explain these events, and the "style" and form of a culture. One more social expression of the symbolic—the one that ties together these others—is the nonverbal; it is the means by which a culture projects the invisible drama onto a literal stage and does so without making the drama explicit.

Clothing, buildings, gestures and oral inflections—all examples of nonverbal material—are a part of a grammar of meaning. But unlike verbal grammars, nonverbal meaning is transmitted through form, not through content. Because of this, the nonverbal is neither discursive nor logical; it is presentational. Put more impressionistically, the communication of nonverbal meaning occurs as an exchange of portraits or performances. Hence, nonverbal meaning is not communicated, as we often assume meaning must be, through the accumulation and logical connection of sequences of ideas. The operating principle at work here is: "We are what we do." This disavowal of the discursive and the logical makes the nonverbal appear far too limited to be taken seriously as an effective language system. But despite this, it can be (and is) a very powerful means of persuasion and coercion.

Since the nonverbal has no tangible argument, one cannot argue with it: there is nothing to disprove. And because its meaning cannot be paraphrased, it is difficult to destroy; one either employs it or one does not. It must be taken whole, complete and intact. For these reasons, the medium of the nonverbal is an effective way for a culture to train its young and to transmit its symbolic meanings. It provides a kind of cultural mirror; as one stands before it, one duplicates what one sees. These acts of duplication are both acts of communication and assertions of community; one not only exchanges information but also indicates that one wishes (or needs) to belong.

This process of duplication requires participation that is visible and concrete. But although its literalness links it with aesthetic reality, certain distinctions must be made. The aesthetic is above all a drama with a form that is clearly a statement. And participation in the aesthetic is something the actor is, on some level, aware of. The nonverbal, on the other hand, depends upon participation but does not make one conscious of oneself in the midst of acting nor aware of the symbolic values one's nonverbal language expresses. This is a difficult distinction to make; because the nonverbal is concrete, we often assume it is explicit—that it is what its form says it is. That this is not the case becomes clear when one recognizes that nonverbal forms change their values when we become aware of them, when we are conscious of using them.

What confuses matters even more is that dramas which are apparently aesthetic may offer both explicit and nonverbal forms of participation. Thus, one may enact a drama, wear a specific and labeling costume and strike a pose, knowing all the time what these forms are supposed to mean, yet be involved *within* another drama of participation whose forms and values remain invisible. To show how this is so, let us demonstrate this point by using a literary example, *Oedipus Rex*, a play whose very structure and meaning depends upon the tension between these two types of participation. The character Oedipus Rex knows he is in a drama of judgment and purgation as king and of self-discovery as an individual, but he cannot see that this very drama is the process by which he becomes culpable. This latter drama is one no one *within* the play can be successfully articulate about; only the *total* presentation of Oedipus' actions and statements can express it. Hence the incredible irony and suspense of *Oedipus Rex*, no matter how many times it is seen or read. To return to the context of German culture: the German soldier going to battle as a knight to defend the kingdom could not recognize that this role belied its "adult" character—that his nonverbal forms of participation happened to assert childhood rather than adulthood.

It should now be obvious that the nonverbal shares much with the symbolic in their common reliance upon mute and unself-conscious forms to transmit meaning and reproduce social values. And the fact that the nonverbal is tangible, in the way the symbolic is not, makes it a valuable aid in exposing the meanings and values that remain invisible and silent.

The German nonverbal material selected as the basis for the following discussion is entirely visual. Oral inflection, intonations and other kinds of oral patterns, like those of music, have been excluded. This was necessary, first, because satisfactory reproduction would have been difficult and, then, because analysis of oral structure would have entailed the elaboration of a complex descriptive system—one similar to that required for structural linguistics. Besides, the virtue of the visual is that it is almost wholly effective on its own terms, especially in a society like the present, which is, as McLuhan has observed, predominantly visual. Consequently, the material has been culled from illustrations, photographs, faces on coins, cartoons, portraits of officials, greeting cards and other such examples from the popular culture.

A study of the visual material of Germany reveals almost immediately the explicit myth of the feudal kingdom. But the variations within the German version of this drama are significant, for they expose a different pattern than one would expect. All visions of the feudal kingdom do not, for instance, present a world in conflict; there are, after all, Camelots. However, in the German image of the kingdom, one discovers continual competition and tension between the various planes of the art: stark opposed to soft; light to dark; and pastoral to industrial (Plates 2, 3, 10, 25 and 42).

Even the more basic German plot of being under siege is not in general outline uniquely German. This plot is widely shared and is built into a number of cultural myths. But when other cultures—the American is a good example—feel vulnerable, the symbol for the state becomes the family; this is the atomic and essential unit of the community, which promises, through its indivisibility, continuity between generations. The soldier—again in the American version—is a son away from home who knows that he bears his family name. The state during wartime is represented by its First Family, whose members stand for the home front, opening their homes to tender care for the wounded who have returned, making bandages with maternal concern, tending to the business of producing supplies for the front, yet always worried about the son they may have to sacrifice in battle.

But this vision of family is missing in the visual representation of the German drama (Plates 98 and 101). The German family when it does appear is not presented as a total generative entity. One does not find examples of all the generational levels within the family—father, mother, children and grandparents—thus suggesting a past and future growing from the family. The family in the German context is not the perpetuating agent of the culture. The symbolic identity of the traditional family characters has been changed. Fathers, by and large, do not exist; nor do mothers as wives. The child, instead of being defined by the family, defines the family, and he serves as the representative of the state within the family rather than the expression of the family to the state (Plates 59, 61, 72 and 77). In sum, the German version of this drama makes the state the symbol for the family rather than the converse, the family a symbol of the state.

In its working of the siege drama, Germany changed the roles of the traditional family members by creating different identities along new divisions. There were, first and most primarily, the knights—those who repel the attack—played by both men and women, children and adults. This is an ageless and functional identity that makes all within it equal; it is also a completely public role (Plates 54 through 86). Women, as we have noted, exist without their husbands. They appear in several guises. Erik Erikson during his analysis of Hitler's childhood* lists two: the first is "the loving, childlike, and slightly martyred cook who belongs in the warm and cozy background," what we have called in the visual material the aunt or Big Bertha (Plates 102 through 106). The second is "the gigantic marble or iron virgin, the monument to the ideal," who on the battlefield often became a version of the female warrior (Plates 87 through 97). There is also a third role for the woman, designed to make her into a backdrop or prop: the role of maiden. Not a wife, she was passive and pure—the one to be protected (Plates 107 through 116).

What is striking in this myth of the feudal kingdom is that, generally speaking, there was no role for the father. Men were either knights or they were grandfathers.

* Childhood and Society (New York: W. W. Norton, 1963), p. 338.

The role of father was clearly one to be distrusted. The fathers in a culture are, after all, the ones responsible for the operation of the society; they are the ones who have brought the present state of affairs about. For the men of Hitler's generation especially, their fathers were the guilty ones—those who had brought Germany to its knees. They were the petty officials who had compromised Germany's ideals by being weak in the time of Germany's trial. The grandfather, on the other hand, represented the myth of a guiltless and honorable past. In the case of Hitler's generation the figure quite specifically recalled the attempts of both Bismarck and Wilhelm II to create a unified and strong Germany and also recalled the early victories of Hindenburg in World War I (Plates 126 through 135). These images are, of course, more mythic statement than factual truth. But as we indicated earlier, by maintaining the image of a past Germany which was honorable, noble and successful, the Germans could retain the nostalgia for a past that had been betrayed.

In a discussion of symbolic drama, distortions, variations and exceptions can be as instructive as versions of the ideal. For example, while the presentation of a total German family is rare in popular German art (and then only as a family out of the mythic past), the Jew is often seen with his family arranged in a complete hierarchy of generations (Plates 117 through 125). In such pictures, the Jewish family composes a lecherous and perverse tableau, suggesting the corrupt (and corrupting) world of the incestuous. It is not surprising that the distaste and ambivalence many Germans felt toward the traditional —private as opposed to public—family form should be projected upon the group that had been selected as the receptacle for all hatreds. The position of the Jewish family as the symbol for corruption and disease within the German society takes on more meaning (and no little irony) if one remembers that the Jew had historically defined himself through his family—and had survived because of it. Now the traditional values of this hierarchical family were inverted, transformed into a negative image and used as one of the justifications for the destruction of the Jew. For the average German with his suspicion of the traditional family, this vision of the diseased family was, from all points of view, both satisfying and reassuring. For the official or popular artist, it was shrewd and reinforcing propaganda.

Two variations of the ideal knight, worth looking at, lay open the delicate tension under which the German drama of feudal kingdom operated: the image of the knight as child and that of the knight as homosexual. To understand how these work, we must return to the basic attribute of the role of knight—the one-dimensionality that defined its actors almost totally in terms of what they did and how they behaved. Such a role, both functional and outer-directed, placed extreme strains upon the individuals employing it. They had continually to be in a state of performance because the knight's role was always a public one. For a culture to be able to use this kind of role without at the same time developing uncontrollable, internal tensions, it must build into its drama certain types of permissible deviations from the primary role that reduce the burdens and strains of continual public performance. This Germany did.

Frequently one finds the knight or soldier turned into a child in contexts which seem, from outside the culture, strangely grotesque. An instance of this is the toilet humor of the German soldier (Plates 79 through 83). On one level, certainly, one can talk of these examples of graffiti as indications of the anal fantasies that seem classic to totalitarian imaginations. In this light, the graffiti serve as psychological keys to the German attitude toward death, repression and work; they indicate the terms in which sublimation is defined in a society based so completely upon the concept of "duty." They are of a piece with the German fascination with manufactured reality and with detailed documentation of its products and history.

What is noteworthy, though, about German graffiti is that they were unblushingly and publicly exhibited. They were not secret and anonymous scrawlings on toilet walls; they were produced as postcards that were openly mailed and were the basis for political satire and humor, often directed at the German soldier himself rather than at his enemy. One way to explain this is to see that the role of soldier-knight was essentially a role patterned after the qualities of the child. In this way we can see that the knight is not, through these postcards, turned into a child —losing his manhood in the process—but that instead he has always been a child, a role that has none of the pejorative connotations of childishness. It is the child who can play with costumes and disguises, tentatively defining himself by them and, thus, experimenting with identities and trying out future roles without feeling restricted or guilty. His world of masquerade is total play, for it exists outside of history and without consequence.

These characteristics of the child were entirely appropriate to serve as a pattern for the German drama; in fact, they made possible the drama itself—the ability to live in an aesthetic reality with roles functionally defined. The role of knight is not only based upon this functional definition but is also the best expression of the child's masquerade imagination in play. The child's use of disguises springs from innocence; it does not carry with it an awareness of the consequences of time or the historical implications of any role, either as that role may imply and determine a personal future or a public national destiny.

Still the adult can never really be innocent. Even though he takes on a role that is similar in outline and motivation to one a child might have, he is lost in experience. At the very most, the adult only has a form of pseudo innocence—unself-consciousness. The child may know what he is doing, but he does not have to be responsible for it; his acts do not affect his "self," since they are only a part of the "role" he is playing. Of course, as we have suggested, such role-playing does define and shape "self"; but those who enter into it need not admit this to themselves. They do not have to feel guilt.

The Nazis, understanding the basic similarities between "unself-consciousness" and "innocence," constructed an equation between child and knight. In doing this, the Nazis made the role of child equivalent to the public role of knight. Both the child and the knight became coequal symbols for the state (Plates 60 and 61). Such an equation had two virtues: it made accessible the role of soldier to children and it allowed adults to participate guiltlessly in the drama of the state, "to act under orders" without feeling connected to (or responsible for) what they did or saw.

The role of homosexual as the German soldier used it is only another example of the child's masquerade in operation. Until one sees this, one may be surprised by the particularly cavalier spirit of the German homosexual's self-portrait; the poses do not threaten his knighthood (Plates 84 through 86). Both the knight-soldier and the homosexual "in drag" share a similar base. Like the role of knight, this homosexuality is a functional identity based upon the reality of disguises. This homosexual world is one of theater with identities achieved by a manipulation of surfaces; men become women as they are able to make up to look like women, effectively imitating their style, bearing and mannerisms.

A reality based upon masquerade is sexually egalitarian; not only can knights play at being women but women can also play at being knights, neither variation regarded as abnormal either to the individual or the public. The role of knight, then, provided for Germans a sufficiently mythic and, thus, impersonal social identity. It was able to encompass a great many variations and levels of society within it and still not betray the individuals who used it. Hence it was an ideal overarching role for a society searching for a public national drama that would consolidate private identities and diminish personal ambivalences.

In an analysis of visual material, if one bears in mind the principles governing nonverbal and symbolic communication, the literal or explicit content of images or scenes is only of secondary importance. For this reason, when the plates were assembled for this study, distinctions were rarely made between satiric, humorous or serious representations, or between art that was intentionally or unintentionally propagandistic. Similarly it made no difference in our arrangement if art had been produced by the left or right, for it was clear that no matter what the political affiliation, the forms of the culture all sustained and reinforced the central myth—that of the feudal kingdom. The only observable major difference between the visual materials of the right and left was one of tonal emphasis: the right created powerful models to portray optimism and heroism even in the midst of destruction; the left used the same powerful figures to portray heroic despair (Plates 98 and 101).

In the collection and analysis of these pictures, our first concern was with the context the image created for itself as an immediate and self-sufficient statement. (What are the meaning and values of one image?) Here one must examine individual figures and objects in order to see how they are presented. One must view clothing as if it were costume, architecture as if it were solely designed as backdrop and objects (guns, planes, horses, etc.) as if they were only props. It was necessary to consider the bearing and gestures of men. And it was also useful to guess at the kind of material houses and buildings were made of, or what it was to seem they were made of, and to see how they were put together, to notice their proportions, and so forth.

On the level of technical execution, the perspective or point of view of the pictures was studied. For instance in taking photographs, did the photographer use a low eye level or a high one, and to what effect? Also examined were the use of lighting and shadows; the use of space, the distance between the foreground and the background; and the effect of cropping—what was included, what had been excluded and why.

Finally we looked to see if an artist relied upon visual clichés that have a wider currency than those which are purely German. On one hand, there were artists who blended into their work visual patterns and textures from classical Western art. An example is the German photographer who used as the composing axis of his photograph the pastoral style of Millet's French Romanticism. In the foreground of his picture is a peasant in the pose of Millet's sower; in the background, a factory is placed against the horizon as in a Romantic painter's gothic conception of a distant, looming castle. What is distinctive in this picture is that, despite its Romantic ancestry, nature is not threatened by industrialization. A castle takes shape out of the smoke of the factory, and the farmer seems no less safe sowing in front of these new walls than he was in the older, agrarian, feudal world. The picture recognizes the power of this new force; in fact, the factory appears to engender itself out of the shrouds of smoke it produces. Nevertheless, the agrarian life remains untouched; it is an image of continued tranquillity. The general effect of the photograph is to include both the farmer and the industrial reality in the creative, yet polarized harmony of the German version of the Romantic myth (Plate 3).

On the other hand, there were artists who restricted themselves to distinctly German images when more common and universal visual clichés were available. The presentation of the mother figure, for example, tended to be bold, drawn with harsh lines and often out of proportion to the rest of the picture in a way that made the children by comparison seem dwarfed, diminished and isolated—this instead of the more traditional soft and balanced composition unifying mother and child (Plate 101).

After one had determined what each specific frame showed, it was then necessary to compare one series of images with another in order to see what forms, shapes and techniques they had in common. Here it became possible to fix the larger context, or drama, that gave the individual frames meaning. It was apparent, for instance, that Bismarck, Wilhelm II, Hindenburg, Hitler and popular drawings of the knight shared many of the same gestures, positions and often even the same facial expressions and lines about the mouth (Plates 48, 49, 50, 52, 55, 129 and 131). Image after image had forms reminiscent of the feudal romance: buildings that looked like castles (Plates 10 and 14); houses that looked like peasant cottages (Plates 21 and 24); turbine factories that looked like fortresses (Plate 4); field whorehouses that looked like medieval icon wagons (Plates 17 and 28); and processions of flags and fields of tents that recalled chivalric lists (Plate 42). In the figure that represented the knight, one found that the eye level was often low, requiring the viewer to look up into the picture and, thus, up at the knight (Plates 54, 60, 65 and 66). The clothing of an individual acting the role of knight, even when it was relatively contemporary, was drawn or photographed to look stiff, shiny and inflexible as if it were armor (Plates 1, 36 and 55); in some cases, when the material worn was soft, the posture and bearing of the figure was itself stiff and bent, as if the soldier were encased in armor (Plates 45 and 70).

IV Art and Propaganda: Making a Reality

By the time one has finished looking through the visual material of Germany, especially that of Hitlerian Germany, it is difficult not to be struck by its documentary clarity. One sees its pronounced visual texture and the planes of shadows that indicate three-dimensional space. In the perception of this documentary sheen, we are faced, once again, with the aesthetic sensibility at work on the surface of reality.

One remembers here the elaborate expense of energy, imagination and technological skill that was invested by the Germans in the documentation of their national experience—an expense that became more elaborate as Germany moved toward a totalitarian state. In one way their immense amount of visual documentary material simply suggests what we have contended earlier: that the Germans could never quite trust their national reality until it had been reaffirmed by an image they could visualize. But their use of the documentary style also reveals the clear understanding the Germans—in particular Hitler and Goebbels—had of the close connection between propaganda and visual matter. At the same time, their use of the documentary reflects the important contribution Germany made to the aesthetic principles of modern propaganda.

By being able to superimpose, for instance, the documentary style upon the visual displays of Nazi public celebrations, Hitler and Goebbels had at their disposal the authority of the documentary's objective and impersonal voice—a voice that ostensibly is so detached and impersonal that it is voiceless. Thus pseudo events like the Nuremberg Party Convention of 1934, presented in Leni Riefenstahl's film *Triumph of the Will,* although in themselves staged propaganda dramas, were made over into real historical events. Generally speaking, they were "real" because they were given the weight and substance that documentary style is able to provide.

But the process of constructing the credibility of a documentary can be a subtle one. *Triumph of the Will* is a good case in point. The Nazis called the convention with an eye to constructing an event that would have the permanence of history even as it was unfolding for the first time. To envision such an event requires an imagination which is able to picture the event *in advance* as if it were already history—that is, to see it as if it had already been documented. As Kracauer observes, "the Convention was planned not only as a spectacular mass meeting, but also as spectacular film propaganda."* For this reason it is difficult to locate the "true" event. How does one determine the true historical event when all the layers and perceptions of the event—including the production of the film—compose the event? For that matter, what does it mean to talk of "documentary credibility" in such a case? The completed film is as much a "fact" in the event as were those who participated. Perhaps the film is even more important than the participants, since its aesthetic requirements determined what the participants would do. One might say that it was, in fact, only with the completion and exhibition of the film that the event finally came into existence.

Triumph of the Will is an elaborate lamination consisting of surfaces upon surfaces—facts upon facts, events upon events—with each surface refracting the meaning of the surfaces beneath it. To begin at any one level is something of an arbitrary act, since each level is defined by the levels above and below it. However, for the moment, let us disregard the film as film in order to reconstruct what the camera itself saw. When we witness the "event" in place of the camera, we discover that we are looking at little but a series of aesthetic forms composed of the members of the Nazi party who were in

---

* Siegfried Kracauer, *From Caligari to Hitler* (Princeton, N.J.: Princeton University Press, 1947), p. 301.

attendance. They have been arranged and ordered so that we cannot help but be conscious of the artificiality of their stance. In addition if we had been in Nuremberg at the time of the convention, we would have witnessed carefully orchestrated choral recitatives, elaborately choreographed parades—one lasted for five hours without a break in the precision—and, finally, the obviously staged illuminations of lights. What we would have seen is one human tableau after another.

Of course, it is always clear to the viewer—when he sees this event by watching the film—that all these effects have been arranged with the camera in mind. And this awareness explains, perhaps, the uneasiness felt by contemporary audiences when they viewed this film. As Kracauer contends: "The deep feeling of uneasiness *Triumph of the Will* aroused in unbiased minds originates in the fact that before our eyes palpable life becomes an apparition—a fact the more disquieting as this transformation affected the vital existence of people. . . . This film represents an inextricable mixture of a show simulating reality and of German reality maneuvered into a show. . . ."* But we miss the point and strategy of this film if we stop with this, assuming that the Nazi propagandists did not wish the German audience to recognize this very same thing: that the film (and the original staging, for that matter) was exactly this—"a show simulating reality and . . . German reality maneuvered into a show."

To achieve this recognition, the film first presents its audience with a transparently artificial overlay of aesthetic forms which organized the human participants. There could be no doubt for the audience that what it was viewing were actors functioning within a role, rather than independent and autonomous human beings. Thus although the German audience might have started watching this film thinking it was going to see the "reality" of fellow Germans at a party convention, the effect of this layer of the film was to displace the expectations of "reality," persuading the audience that what it was seeing was in some way unreal.

To make an audience aware of the unreal when it views "reality," or what normally passes for its reality, is the true cutting edge of the propagandist's skill. He has understood the first tenet of the modern sensibility—and of modern art. (The "modern," for our purposes, is not simply the contemporary; it is continuous with the sensibility projected by writers like Machiavelli and Castiglione—those who wrote that peculiarly modern genre of tracts, the "how-to" books: "How to Be a Prince"; "How to Be a Courtier.") As we have seen, Henry James expressed this modern sensibility most succinctly: "It is art that *makes* life, makes interest, makes importance. . . ." What links the propagandist's art to that of James is their common understanding that without the form of art there can be no reality, or to say it another way, there can be no perception of a reality.

The awareness of "unreality" engendered by the German propagandists is an awareness that springs from a consciousness of forms. It is an awareness that fortifies the belief in a reality which exists only when it can be examined as form. This is to subscribe to a reality that is all composition, all structure. But this kind of awareness, rather than diminishing the sense of reality, reasserts it all the more.

On this point: A. J. Liebling, an American journalist, remarked once in a dispatch sent from the German

* *Caligari*, p. 303.

front that a battle never seemed more "real" than when it evoked the memory of some John Wayne movie he had seen. This sensation is similar to what the tourist feels when he visits the Grand Canyon and finds that the scene is ready-made for his camera. As often as not, faced with such a prospect, he will write home on a picture postcard: "How picturesque it all is." By that he means two things: how like a picture *and* how real. Both meanings are true. The scene is real; and his camera—a device we use to authenticate—will document its reality. And of course, the scene is also ready-made; after all, it does appear on the obverse side of his postcard.

This tourist finds himself in a position parallel to the one Liebling found himself in, although the tourist may not be as aware of its restrictions and liabilities as was Liebling. He is a camera, a camera programed to take pictures of scenes he has been taught to recognize. And it will be impossible for him to recognize, appreciate or photograph any others. They simply do not exist since they cannot be perceived. (Taking this perceptual dilemma into account, Oscar Wilde quite correctly, albeit sardonically, observed that "the first duty of life is to be as artificial as possible." A writer like Henry James—and here one might add Flaubert—and propagandists like Riefenstahl can be said to hold a view that extends without distorting the logic of Wilde's epigram: the first duty of the artist is to make life as artificial as possible in order to make its reality, or a reality, more apparent.)

The effect of establishing a sense of the unreal in the audience of *Triumph of the Will* was to saturate that audience with forms, so that it could not escape the feeling that if there were no forms there could be no reality and no meaning. José Ortega y Gasset describes a similar effect when he writes: "The beauty of a painting does not consist in the fact, which is of no importance so far as the painting is concerned, that it causes us pleasure, but on the contrary we begin to think it a beautiful painting when we become conscious of the gently persistent demand it is making on us to feel pleasure."* This "gently persistent demand" is the power of the form upon us, and its power to make us feel or see is what draws our attention and validates its "reality." The beauty of art, or any form, is our recognition of this power. Our awe—and in some cases our fear—springs from its mastery over our feelings; our delight and fascination, from its ability to make us see.

It is this power of forms to which Riefenstahl pays tribute (and it explains both her title and technique) in *Triumph of the Will.* The German will, and identity, has finally emerged triumphant, ready to translate itself; it is now ready to master political reality. But this was only possible after Germany had discovered its form, its way of becoming visualizable. Hitler and the Nazi aesthetic provided this form; it is this discovery and its implementation which Riefenstahl "documents."

Her film, as it praises and renders the forms of the Nazi imagination, is also an encomium to propaganda. Again we find that the film delivers its praise on several levels. Within the film, Goebbels reminds his audience (both that of the convention and that of the film) of the virtues and successes of Nazi propaganda, thus praising the propaganda successes of the very spectacle he is participating in. Goebbels sees propaganda as a deep and unifying victory for the German people; it is not to him

* *The Modern Theme,* trans. James Cleugh (New York: Harper & Row, 1961), p. 45. Reprinted by permission of Revista de Occidente, S.A., Madrid.

a devious or shabby political tool of the state that one must hide from the people. It is to be embraced. Riefenstahl, in re-presenting the aesthetic form of the convention within the aesthetic form of the film, celebrates not only the successes of the German will, Goebbels' propaganda and the party convention but also the success of her own film as propaganda. This film is, itself, an *exemplum* of the will triumphant.

As our discussion of *Triumph of the Will* shows, to be caught up in an awareness of forms is to become increasingly engrossed in the details that make up these forms. Here a film like *Triumph* betrays its connection to the aesthetic traditions of surrealism and Dada art. Detail after detail accumulates; reality made unreal is supersaturated and intensified documentary realism. All of these—realism, surrealism and the documentary—depend upon the ability to reinforce a pattern of thought (one that post-Cartesian man is particularly susceptible to) which holds that whatever one sees clearly and distinctly must be true and, therefore, must also be real. When this inclination to accept a universe of details as real is merged with art that deliberately manufactures artifice, reality and pseudo reality become equivalent. An imitation Grand Canyon will do as well as the real thing—whatever the "real" thing, at this point, can be said to be. (Disneyland draws as many tourists sending postcards home as does the Grand Canyon; and what is more important, postcards from each probably say the same thing —how picturesque!) The result of this—be it through Riefenstahl's form or Disney's—is that one is no longer able to apprehend or perceive the existence of the fluid process we sometimes call reality, since it has no form and thus has no way of making itself visible.

One further consequence of the propagandist's strategy needs to be considered. By helping to speed up the process by which the artificial is made real, the propagandist has helped to change the subject matter and the position of the historian. The simple act of reporting makes an event where none existed, and as a result we seem to lose our grasp on the notion of objectivity. What do we mean by the concept of "documentary" in the propagandist's world, where the only thing that can be documented is the artificial or theatrical event? In short, could Leni Riefenstahl have "documented" the Nuremberg Convention in any other way? Was there a non-artificial reality beneath the surface which would have remained nonartificial even after it was enclosed in her form?

These questions suggest a distinction, perhaps worth making, between a *document*, in itself a concrete fact that can be located in time, and a *documentary*, which is essentially the product of an act whose purpose is to make something *seem* concrete. The first exists no matter how one interprets it; the second can only be an interpretation no matter how concrete the surface it offers.

Especially as the documentary has the authority of technological "objectivity" (that is, impartiality) furnished by the media of film and, in the last two decades, television, the documentary is primarily a visual art; it is no longer a dimension of the historian's craft. Its audience can be persuaded by the style of what it sees, the details of form that indicate authenticity, rather than being persuaded by the content of its narrative.

This emphasis of form connects the documentary to nonverbal language; like the nonverbal, it shows "truth" through the process of presenting itself. It cannot argue or discuss its point. We are sometimes apt to forget the basically nonverbal nature of the documentary, since it often appears to be so completely explicit and discursive. But its discursive appearance can be deceptive. For instance, what we usually receive when watching a television documentary, or newscast, is not the news but the style and form of authenticity: and we ourselves learn from it how to sound and how to look reliable.

One thing we can learn from German propaganda—perhaps worth pondering—is that the artificial texture of its documentaries is precisely what makes them seem true (that is, "reliable") renderings of reality. This is a major contribution to the craft of the propagandist—he need no longer cover his tracks; in fact, by revealing them, he earns for himself and his product new credibility. But this approach has implications that extend beyond the confines of strictly political manipulations. It forces us to reconsider the way in which we understand concepts like "reality," "truth" and "meaning" and also makes it necessary to re-examine the nature of perception. The principle behind German propaganda is a singular one: that the degree to which we accept something as true depends not upon its "naturalness" but upon the exact opposite, an extreme "unnaturalness."

The principle of "unnaturalness" may have for its purpose an intent quite different from that of the totalitarian mind. Rather than reinforce views of reality, it may wish to do the opposite: to satirize and ridicule the standard vision of reality, doing this in order to expose the "grotesque" logic of the social system. We are faced with a very complex problem because the only thing that distinguishes the totalitarian from the satirist is that the satirist is by fate—or by numbers—outside the society and in the minority. His art is propaganda, but it appears less virulent because its purpose is to inoculate the system by producing a minor version of the mass infection. But what if the satirist's view becomes the Establishment's view? If his larger-than-life reproductions become the norm for reality? If his technique of distortions becomes the technique of mass propaganda? How, then, is his approach different?

To put this in perspective, let us look at the work of certain Dadaists. Hugo Ball, an early and important Dadaist, wrote in his diary of the effect of some experiments in theater, mime and masks created by Marcel Janco.

> Janco has made a number of masks for the new show, which bear the marks of something more than talent. They recall the Japanese or Ancient Greek theater, and yet they are wholly modern. They are designed to make their effect at a distance, and in the relatively small space of the cabaret the result is astonishing. We were all there when Janco arrived with the masks, and each of us put one on. The effect was strange. Not only did each mask seem to demand the appropriate costume; it also called for a quite specific set of gestures, melodramatic and even close to madness. Although five minutes earlier none of us had had the remotest idea of what was to happen, we were soon draped and festooned with the most unlikely objects, making the most outlandish movements, each out-inventing the other. The dynamism of the masks was irresistible. In one moment we became aware of the

great importance of such masks in mime and drama. The masks simply demanded that their wearers should start up a tragic-absurd dance. What fascinates us about these masks is that they represent, not humanity, but characters and emotions that are larger than life. The paralysing horror which is the backcloth of our age is here made visible.*

Written about 1916, during the First World War but before Hitler, by one of a group of artists (Marcel Janco was also an early Dadaist) whose purpose was the very opposite of Hitler's, there can be no little irony in the way their aesthetic principles were turned around: using the same method, Hitler transmuted a vision of paralysis into the reality of action; horror was horror no more, the outlandish was now a dramatization of reality.

A film like *Triumph of the Will* and what it photographs is the culmination of a long search for a coherent form and a coherent German identity. One way to understand Germany's history and its fascination with borders, frames and boundaries is to see this search as a series of aesthetic operations in which limits (that is, forms) were continually being drawn. The object of all this "drawing" was to exclude that which was not German and, thereby, create the perfect outline of the "true German."

* Quoted in Hans Richter, *Dada: Art and Anti-Art* (New York: McGraw-Hill, 1966), p. 23. Reprinted by permission of the publisher. All rights reserved.

The theory at work here is that if one can exclude a sufficient amount of the non-German, one will ultimately come upon a definition which will say what it is *to be* German. But as can be seen, this process starts with negative space and negative definitions: the exclusion of what one is *not*, or senses one is not, rather than a positive set of definitions of what one is.

As the first step in this process of exclusion, Germany under Bismarck drew its feudal boundaries around one nation. Once this had been reasonably successful, Germany started to draw circles, such as Bismarck's Kulturkampf, within the German community itself in order to drain off the un-German characteristics. Each of these stages had a limited success, but *the* German was still not defined. The positive definition seemed always just beyond the present set of distinctions; and since, as we have argued, the Germans could not be satisfied by a negative series of definitions, they continued to pursue the course of boundary-making until they could hear the click of absolute certainty and absolute meaning. When Bismarck's centripetal system of consolidation proved unsatisfactory, Wilhelm's solution was to expand the circle into a new imperialism: the vision of a pan-Germany. Hitler's solution was to fuse the two systems; he tried both expansionism and concentration—the imperialism of his Aryan Germany and the concentration of his concentration camps. While it lasted, this double helix provided a satisfactory conclusion to the German search for identity through the search for form, a search that moves *between* a perception of what one is not and what one is.

a. Artists have recognized that the expressive power of their works is dependent upon their creating a world set apart from the one in which the audience lives and breathes, so that the spectators may find it easier to engage themselves with the artistic symbols.

Murray Edelman

b. The tree will have developed gloriously and before it the German Michael will be standing, his hand upon his sword, and looking out into the distance in order to protect it. That peace stands firm under the shield and under the sword of the German Michael.

Wilhelm II

1.

A Discourse Through Pictures

A Note on Reading the Visual Material

Although the best way to see a picture is to look at it individually—for itself and by itself, noting the idiosyncrasies that make it unique—to understand uniqueness, one must also be able to place individual examples within a larger continuum. An individual gesture will make no sense unless one has seen the gesture in a number of different situations which expose its meaning and implications. The grammar of gestures is very much like the grammar of language: meaning accumulates with an increased experience with different patterns of usage.

On the other hand, too long or elaborate a continuum of images distracts one's attention. One does not see, if one is bombarded by a multitude of frames, small but important variations or embellishments. In addition, a system that is too completely integrated and interconnected leads the reader's eye, persuading him to see what might not be there or diminishing his ability to see connections for himself which the system-maker could not perceive.

At best, the following organization of pictures is an uneasy compromise between two strong desires: the first, to make each picture "speak" for itself while at the same time providing a context which will help correlate and interrelate what one "hears"; and the second, to avoid a prefabricated visual experience which would predetermine what the reader can see.

To make this compromise work, we have organized pages as self-contained frames in which individual pictures relate to each other through common, easily located gestures and themes. In order to suggest variations, we arranged individual images on any one page in both vertical and horizontal progression. Thus by starting from any one image, the reader may immediately see variations and alterations within a limited focus. This approach means that one may read down or across a page following particular permutations of a gesture, a dramatic episode or a type of character. Taken together, each set of images outlines one dimension of the German symbolic drama.

Since individual pictures function symbolically on several levels at once, we have tried to isolate and indicate the particular level we were concerned with. But to show how the other levels of the picture work, we have, from time to time, repeated some of the images. This serves to repeat the previous context with its symbolic meaning, hence extending the continuum as one moves along. But such repetitions also serve to show how the meaning of nonverbal material changes in emphasis and value as the context and frame are changed.

Analyzing the nonverbal, then, is much like using a microscope; each setting exposes a different slice of the total structure. No one setting is completely right; but then, no one setting is completely wrong. The truth of the whole rests in being able to remember the details of the individual layers while trying to reconstruct the total structure from which the slices have been cut.

Outline of Visual Material

<table>
<tr><td>The Scene</td><td>Plates</td></tr>
<tr><td>The Castle and the Cottage</td><td></td></tr>
<tr><td> 1. To the scale of the heroic: a feudal kingdom in concrete</td><td>2–14</td></tr>
<tr><td> 2. To the scale of the personal: the peasant myth</td><td>15–25</td></tr>
<tr><td> 3. To the scale of the secular: the religious as political proscenium</td><td>26–32</td></tr>
<tr><td> 4. To the scale of fantasy: theater as reality</td><td>33–47</td></tr>
<tr><td>The Actors</td><td></td></tr>
<tr><td>The Knight</td><td></td></tr>
<tr><td> 1. Strength</td><td>48–59</td></tr>
<tr><td> 2. Strength, purity</td><td>60–63</td></tr>
<tr><td> 3. Strength, purity, innocence</td><td>64–68</td></tr>
<tr><td> 4. Purity, innocence, youth</td><td>69–74</td></tr>
<tr><td> 5. Innocence, youth</td><td>75–78</td></tr>
<tr><td> 6. Innocence, youth, perverted</td><td>79–83</td></tr>
<tr><td> 7. Perverted</td><td>84–86</td></tr>
<tr><td>The Female Warrior</td><td></td></tr>
<tr><td> 1. Innocence and strength</td><td>87–88</td></tr>
<tr><td> 2. Innocence and strength maintained in the world of the masculine</td><td>89–92</td></tr>
<tr><td> 3. Innocence and strength lost in the world of the masculine</td><td>93–97</td></tr>
<tr><td>The Iron Virgin</td><td></td></tr>
<tr><td> 1. The maternal warrior</td><td>98–101</td></tr>
<tr><td> 2. The aunt</td><td>102–106</td></tr>
<tr><td>The Maiden</td><td></td></tr>
<tr><td> 1. Snow White and Rose Red</td><td>107–116</td></tr>
<tr><td>The Dwarf</td><td></td></tr>
<tr><td> 1. Among knights</td><td>117–118</td></tr>
<tr><td> 2. The corruption of gold</td><td>119–122</td></tr>
<tr><td> 3. Among family</td><td>123–125</td></tr>
<tr><td>The Domestic Warrior</td><td></td></tr>
<tr><td> 1. The grandfather</td><td>126–135</td></tr>
</table>

The Scene

The Castle and the Cottage   1. to the scale of the heroic:
a feudal kingdom in concrete

2.

3.

The Scene

The Castle and the Cottage   1. to the scale of the heroic:
a feudal kingdom in concrete

4.

c. For an act of persuasion is
affected by the character of
the scene in which it takes
place and of the agents to
whom it is addressed.

Kenneth Burke

d. Achieved is the glorious work
On mountain height
The hall immortal;
In gorgeous grandeur
Glitter its walls.
As I drew it in dream
As I marked it in mind,
Resplendent and strong
It displays its might:
Lofty, lordly abode!

Wotan, "Ring of the Nibelung"

Hans Poelzig: Wasserturm in Posen. 1911

5.

Peter Behrens: Verwaltungsgebaude der Mannesmannwerke in Dusseldorf. 1912

6.

7.

8.

9.

The Scene

The Castle and the Cottage   1. to the scale of the heroic:
a feudal kingdom in concrete

Ordensburg Vogelsang in der Eifel. Auf den Ordensburgen wird der Führernachwuchs für die Partei erzogen

10.

11.

EIN PLÄTZCHEN AN DER SONNE

1919

1918

JEDEM, DER MIR'S AUCH GÖNNT!

12.

e. Insofar as (men) must do something, rhetoric is unnecessary, its work being done by the nature of things, though often these necessities are not of a natural origin, but come from necessities imposed by man-made conditions, as with the kind of "peithananke" (or compulsion under the guise of persuasion).

Kenneth Burke

13.

Westwall, Packsperre.

14.

Bodo Ebhardt:
Marksburg am Rhein. Beg. 1899

The Scene

The Castle and the Cottage   2. to the scale of the personal:
the peasant myth

f. Symbolization constitutes
objects . . . which would not
exist except for the context
of social relationships
wherein symbolization occurs.

George Herbert Mead

15.

16.

17.

18.

19.

20.

The Castle and the Cottage   2. to the scale of the personal: the peasant myth

g. The homeland, the landscape, the living space, the language community are embodied in the family which roams and grows beyond the borders. In it lives the child with mores and customs, the dialect of the play, of celebration, in it live the song, the fairy tale, the proverb, native costume and furniture and utensils. In it lie the ultimate energies of primordial folk art.

Kurt Karl Eberlein, "Was ist deutsch in der deutschen Kunst?"

Paul Wolf: Siedlung Hannover-Laatzen. 1919/20

1410-1705

Wandmalerei über dem Eingang zum Postamt in Kochel. Reichspostdirektion München Maler Demmel, Königsdork.

The Castle and the Cottage 2. to the scale of the personal: the peasant myth

h. Witnesses of political acts
are likely to be sensitive
to settings and to judge them
as appropriate or inappropriate.

...All have their distinctive
and dramaturgical features,
planned by the arrangers and
actors in the event and ex-
pected by their audiences.

Murray Edelman

23.

Die Wählburg, der schönste deutsche Bauernhof

24.

Die schwäbischen Arbeitsdienſtmänner haben ihr Zelt mit der Faſſade eines
heimatlichen Bauernhauſes ausgebaut

25.

The Castle and the Cottage   3. to the scale of the secular:
the religious as political proscenium

26.

Theodor Fischer: Detail der Schule an der Haimhauser Strasse in München. 1897/98

i. Through the creation of an artificial space a particular set of impressions and responses can be intensified, serving to condense and organize a wide range of connotations, free of the irrelevancies, distractions, and qualifications of which everyday life mainly consists . . . (The creation of such space) involves a corresponding diversion of attention from cognitive and rational analysis.

Murray Edelman

27.

28.

29.

30.

Das Haus der Deutschen Kunst in München

Theodor Fischer:

31.   Garnisonkirche in Ulm. 1908/11

32.

The Castle and the Cottage 4. to the scale of fantasy:
theater as reality

Wachtturm im Lager Langwasser

33.

34.

Zeppelinfeld, Aufmarschgelände in Nürnberg

35.

Martin Dülfer: Theater in Dortmund. 1903/04

The Castle and the Cottage   4. to the scale of fantasy:
theater as reality

Mahnmal an der Feldherrnhalle in München.

37.

Marine-Ehrenmal in Laboe
an der Kieler Förde.

Jäger-Ehrenmal in Bergeinsamkeit
auf dem Grünten:

38.

39.

„Wir waren eins in der Liebe zur Heimat
und haben ihr alles gegeben.
Bruder — wie klein ist dein Streit."

40.

Das Tannenberg-Denkmal, das Wahrzeichen der Befreiung Ostpreußens.

The Castle and the Cottage   4. to the scale of fantasy:
theater as reality

41.

Otto der Große,
der erste Träger der Krone
des altdeutschen Kaiserreiches

j. A yielding to the form
prepares for assent to the matter identified with it.

Kenneth Burke

42.

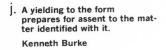

The Castle and the Cottage 4. to the scale of fantasy: theater as reality

43. Luftwaffe und Hakenkreuz

Panzerwagen beim Aufmarsch

44.

45.
Arbeitsdienst (von Ferdinand Staeger)

46.

47.

The Knight 1. strength

No. 39.
XXIX. Jahrg.

8. KRIEGS-NUMMER
LUSTIGE BLÄTTER

Preis:
36 h.

Bis gebeugt am Boden liegen, Führe stolz von Sieg zu Siegen Eingedenk der tapfern Ahnen, Hinter deiner Truppen Fahnen

49.

50.

Kaiser Wilhelm II. als oberster Kriegsherr.

51.

52.

53.

The Knight 1. strength

Mein Volk, wie sie dich hassen,
Ward nie ein Volk gehaßt.
Und will der Ruhm dich kleiden
In deiner Taten Glanz,
Mein Volk, wie sie beneiden
Jed' Blättchen deinem Kranz!

Sie zwangen's mit dem Schwerte,
Daß du in Waffen stehst
Und über rote Erde
Ein Held und Rächer gehst.
Wie wenn die Sklaven meutern,
Und Pöbel-Krieg begann,
Fliegt dich aus Lügen-Schleudern
Der Kot der Gossen an.

Auf die, so schlecht beraten
Sich nach dem Schmutz gebückt,
Wirf' alle Wucht der Taten,
Bis Wahrheit sie erdrückt;

Und Grund zum Hassen haben,
Wie der Besiegte haßt.

Und wenn sie droh'n und keifen
Rings um dein herrlich Land,
So lernst du fester greifen
Nach deines Bruders Hand;
Und fühlst's, daß Starkes, Gutes
Die ernste Stunde spinnt
Denen, die eines Blutes
Und eines Willens sind.

Die Neider, eh' du's dachtest,
Ward dir zu strafen Pflicht —
Doch eh' du sie verachtest,
Vergiß das Eine nicht:
Auch deiner Siege Gassen,
Mein Volk, sind hell und weit
Geebnet durch ihr Hassen,
Gebaut von ihrem Neid! R. P.

54.

55.

My people, how they hate you,
More than any people has ever been
    hated.
Fame wants to clothe you
For the honor of your deeds—
My people, how jealous they are
Of every leaf in your garland.

They forced you with the sword
To take up your arms,
To stride over the red earth
As a hero and an avenger—
And when the slaves rebel
And proletarian war starts,
They will fling lies at you
And their excrement.

Onto those who so ill advisedly
Inclined themselves to smut
Throw all the weight of your deeds,
Until the truth smothers them
And they have reason to hate,
As the Conquered One hates.

And when they threaten you and
    snarl
Around your glorious country,
You will learn to grip more strongly
The hand of your brother;
And feel that strong and good
    things
Are done for those who are of one
    will and one blood.

Those who are jealous,
It is your duty to punish—
But before you disdain them
Do not forget one thing:
The streets of your victory,
My people, are wide and bright
    because their hate has smoothed
    them
And their jealousy paved them!

Translation from German text, Plate 54

56.

Die Tauchbootwaffe. (1. Februar 1917.)   „Fertig! Los!"

57.

Gedenkhalle in Pasewalk

I. Safe is that peace
behind which stands the
German St. Michael with
his shield and his
sword.

Wilhelm II

Der Dienst am Volk

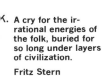

K. A cry for the ir-
rational energies of
the folk, buried for
so long under layers
of civilization.

Fritz Stern

58.

Wehrdienst (Soldat vom Gefallenendenkmal in München von Bernhard Bleeker)

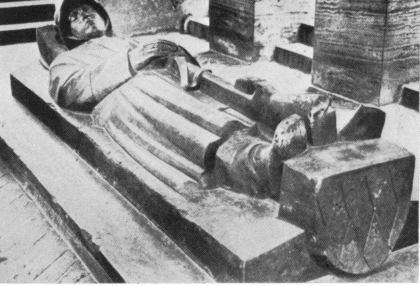

59.

Jugenddienst
(Hitlerjunge von Bernhard Lohf)

60.

61.

Helft uns siegen!

zeichnet
die
Kriegsanleihe

62.

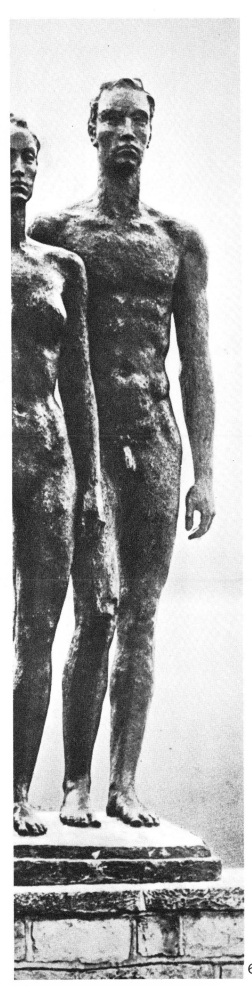

The Knight   3. strength, purity, innocence

The Fashion-Sinner

Michael, have I hurt you?
The cock had such beautiful
      feathers.
The cock in days of peace
Stood so proudly on the Gallic
      garbage pile.
And I, weak as a woman is,
Liked so much to wear colored
      feathers . . .
Michael, a different time came!
Michael you are stiffly dressed in
      iron
And are playing with bloody knives;
Michael, I have made a vow,
Pluck the feathers of that Gallic
      cock.
And look: I will improve!

Translation from German text, Plate 68

Nordische Rasse:
Idealgestalten

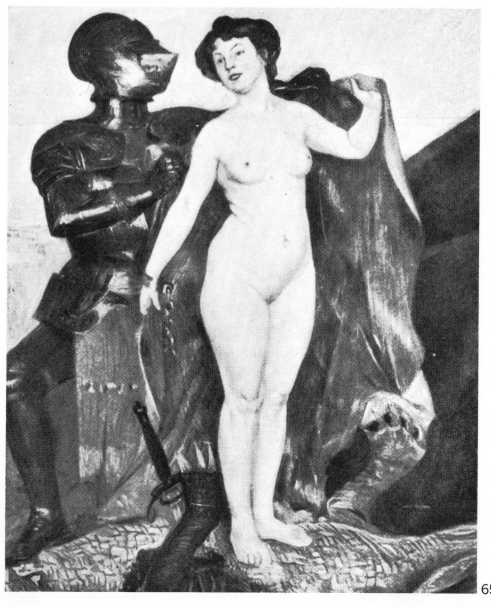

64.
Prinz Eugen

65.

66.
Der Bamberger Reiter,
das Idealbild eines deutschen Kaisers

67.

Zeichnung von Bayros.

68.

Die Mode=Sünderin.

Michel, hab' ich dir weh getan?
So schöne Federn hatte der Hahn,
Der Hahn in friedlichen Tagen —
Er stand so stolz auf gallischem Mist,
Und ich hab', schwach wie ein Weibchen ist,
So gern bunte Federn getragen . . .

Michel, es kam eine andere Zeit!
Michel, du starrst im Eisen=Kleid
Und spielst mit blutigen Messern;
Michel, ich hab' ein Gelübde getan,
Rupf ihn gehörig, den gallischen Hahn,
Und schau': ich will mich bessern! —r.

The Knight   4. purity, innocence, youth

69.

Die Heerführer Wilhelm, Kronprinz des Deutschen Reichs und von Preußen, Führer der 5. Armee.

70.

71.

72.

Prinz Joachim von Preußen in Felduniform, nach seiner Verwundung in die Front zurückkehrend.

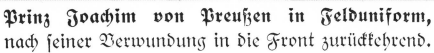

M. Encased in a coat of mail, prepared for battle, the emperor marches past with his renowned generals; the people crowd around him enthusiastically; the swords glitter; "A Stronghold Sure Is Our Lord" is the battle cry which rises above all the din of battle; and, in the folk song "Hail, Hail the Kaiser," the song of triumph reaches its climax. This is genuine German music.

Program for the Kaiser March, produced at Mannheim, 1917

Zeichnung von E. Heilemann.

73.

74.

The Knight   5. innocence, youth

76.

Mädchenmißhandlung im Arbeitshaus von Greifswald
Satir. Zeichnung aus der „Jugend" anläßlich eines dies-
bezüglichen Sensationsprozesses

What Is the German Fatherland?
(A Handy Slogan)

There, there,you naughty children,
you screamers. You disturb the
whole neighborhood with your screams,
screams
that merit a punishment from a
high hand (authority).

Translation from German text, Plate 78

Vor dem Schloß.

Ich stehe vor dem Kaiserschloße,
Das leuchtend ragt in edler Pracht,
Und muſtre ſtolz die Feldgeſchoße,
Die man als Beute heimgebracht.
Ich ſehe Kindergruppen ſchweifen
Um eines Mörſers Eiſenſchlund,
Und zarte Mädchenhände greifen
In des Geſchützes Rieſenmund.

Mein Blick folgt einem hübſchen Kinde,
Ein Sträußchen Blumen zieht's hervor,
Und ſpielend reiht es zum Gewinde
Die Aſtern um das Eiſenrohr . . .
Die Unſchuld liebkoſt die Vernichtung,
Die Einfalt tändelt mit dem Tod —
Und eine ſanfte Friedensdichtung
Keimt plötzlich auf in Nacht und Not.

Oscar Blumenthal.

In Front of the Palace

I stand in front of the palace of the
    Kaiser
That stands in shining splendor,
And proudly look at the captured
    cannon
Brought home as booty.
I see groups of children playing
Around the iron mouth of the
    cannon
And see tender hands of girls
Reach into the giant cannon mouth.

My glance follows a pretty child.
She bears a bunch of flowers
And in play winds it around the
    iron rod.
Innocence embraces destruction.
Ignorance dallies with death—
And a tender poem of peace
Suddenly grows out of the night of
    death.

Translation from German text, Plate 77

77.

Was ist das Deutsche Vaterland?

(Ein unfehlbares Schlagwort.)

Plon-Plon   Frossard   Mac-Mahon.   Es   Sie   Er.

78.   Hessen.   Baden   Würtemberg.   Sachsen.   Bayern   Preussen.

„Da! da! ihr unartige Kinder, ihr Schreihäls, die ganze Nachbarschaft stört ihr mit eurer Schreierei
das verdient eine Züchtigung von hoher Hand!"

The Knight 6. innocence, youth, perverted

Der Maler Michael Biró, der als österreichischer Oberleutnant den Feldzug in Galizien mitmachte, erzählt zu diesem Bilde:

Unser Bataillonskommandant war ein sehr pedantischer Herr, der sich stets darüber aufhielt, daß zahlreiche Ruhrkranke beim Vormarsch zur Verrichtung ihrer Notdurft im Straßengraben zurückblieben. Er beschloß daher zu rationalisieren und gab Befehl: »15 Minuten Rast und alles muß . . . . .« Befehl ist Befehl und so hockte sich das ganze Bataillon nieder. Da es aber den braven Soldaten respektwidrig erschien, bei einer solchen Tätigkeit dem Vorgesetzten das Gesicht zuzuwenden, zeigten sie ihm alle den Hintern.

79.

On Command

(Drawing by Michael Biro)

The painter Michael Biro, who took part in the Gallic campaign as a lieutenant from Austria, tells the following story about this picture:

The commander of our battalion was a very pedantic gentleman who was always being interrupted by the fact that many of the men, who were sick with diarrhea, had to stop in the ditches to obey the call of nature. He therefore decided to order things by giving the command: Halt 15 minutes and everyone shit! A command is a command, and the whole battalion squatted down. As it however seemed disrespectful to turn their faces toward their commander while executing such a lowly function the soldiers all showed him their asses.

Translation from German text, Plate 79

80.

Im Stinkraum ist Gasmaskenprobe —
Die Seewehr fühlt sich wie ein Geck.
Dumpf brummelt wildes Tiergeschnobe,
Nichts ist dagegen Hagenbeck.

81.

Ein Abenteuer auf dem Kriegsschauplatze im Weltkriege

An den bekannten Schüttelreim,
Der oft schon ward belacht
Dem jeden wird bekannt er sein,
Hab neulich ich gedacht.
Als ich im Schützengraben vor Souplet
Geplagt von sogenannter „Diarrhoe"
Frühmorgens auf dem Scheißhaus saß,
Dazu ein liebes Brieflein las
Der Schüttelreim besagt sehr wahr
Ganz unverblümt und offenbar:
„Zum Reisen braucht man Schuhe,
Zum Scheißen braucht man Ruhe"
Wie ich auf den Gedanken kam
Verhält sich so — hört mich mal an:
Ich sass, wie ich schon angeführt
Auf jener Stange ungeniert.
Schiß fort mit voller Jugendkraft,
Was mir im Leib Beschwerde schafft,
Mit Bums und Krach tief in das Loch,
Aus dem es ganz abscheulich roch.
Und tadellos gelang der Schiß
Ganz furchtbar scheißt man b. Kommiß.
Da — plötzlich — ei verflixt noch mal
Da saust mit schrecklichem Skandal,
Mit niederträchtigem Gebrumm
Unheimlich 'ne Granate rum!
Kurz hinterm Scheißhauß schlägt sie ein
Und wühlt ein tiefes Loch hinein
Na, denke ich, was kann das sein,
Für diesmal hattest du noch Schwein.
Und — da's mich noch ein wenig quälte,
Auch nicht am nötgen Nachdruck fehlte
Schiß ich dann seelenruhig fort,
In den dazu bestimmten Ort
Jedoch das Schicksal schreitet schnell,
Herangesaust kam ein Schrapnell;

Und Donnerwetter — sakra bleu —
Unmittelbar in meiner Näh.
Krepiert das niederträcht'ge Aas.
Das war mir wirklich außer'm Spaß,
Denn ohne jeden Zweifel warsch,
Die Ludersch ziel'n nach meinem Arsch,
Der Dreck flog rum, just wie die Spreu
Da wars mit der Geduld vorbei:
Mit einem Satz sprang ich empor,
Daß ich die Stiefel fast verlor,
Die Hosen war'n noch abgeknöpft,
Und renne, bis ich schier erschöpft,
Von dem verflixten Scheißhaus fort,
In meines Erdlochs sichern Ort
Dort habe ich philosophiert,
Den Schüttelreim einmal seziert
Und ward mir völlig drüber klar,
Wie treffend jenes Sprichwort war
Wenn man dagegen nun bedenkt.
Sich in Erinnerung still versenkt
Wie war's doch in der Heimat schön,
Muß man daselbst mal scheißen geh'n,
'ne Zeitung nahm man schnell zur Hand
'ne Zigarett' ward angebrannt
Und seelenruhig — ei der Daus —
Schiß man sich recht gemütlich aus
Drum,wem dies holdeGlück beschieden
Wer scheißen kann, froh u. zufrieden,
Der denke an den Landwehrmann
Der nicht mal ruhig scheißen kann!
Doch wenn der Frieden kommt ins Land
Wir reichen uns die Bruderhand,
Dann fällt in dem Moment uns ein
Der wohlbekannte Schüttelreim:
„Zum Reisen braucht man Schuhe,
Zum Scheißen braucht man Ruhe!"

Die Latrine
Tiefste Erniedrigung als Gegenstand humoristischer Darstellung
Postkarte aus der Sammlung A. Wolff, Leipzig

An Adventure on the Battleground
in the World War

When I was sitting in the shit house in the trenches recently, I thought about the well-known maxim: "To travel one needs shoes, to shit one needs peace." The way I got to thinking about this was this. I was shitting with great vigor and energy into the hole, when a grenade landed right near me. I thought I was lucky it had not hit me and shit merrily on.

Almost at once however a piece of shrapnel almost hit me and I became convinced they were aiming for my ass. I therefore raced for the safety of the trenches without bothering to pull up my pants. There I analyzed the maxim. How lovely it was back home! When you had to take a shit you sat there peacefully with a newspaper and a cigarette. Therefore those of you who shit in peace think of the poor soldier who can't even do that. When peace comes and we extend to each other the hand of Brotherhood, we will think of the maxim "To travel one needs shoes, to shit one needs peace."

Translation from German text, Plate 81

82.

Feldlatrinenordnung von der Westfront
Aus J. C. Brunner, Illustrierte Sittengeschichte

83.

Der Marsch auf Paris
*Erotisch-politische Zeichnung eines deutschen Soldaten,
im Schützengraben entstanden (Marne 1915)*

n. And the old German
virtues now lost were:
childlike simplicity,
subjectivity, individuality.

Fritz Stern

The Knight   7. perverted

o. The youth movement ...
a strong demand
for purity mixed
with a strong
craving for male
companionship.

Fritz Stern

p. In the new Germany
the talents and joys
of the child would be
preserved in the adult.

Fritz Stern

85.

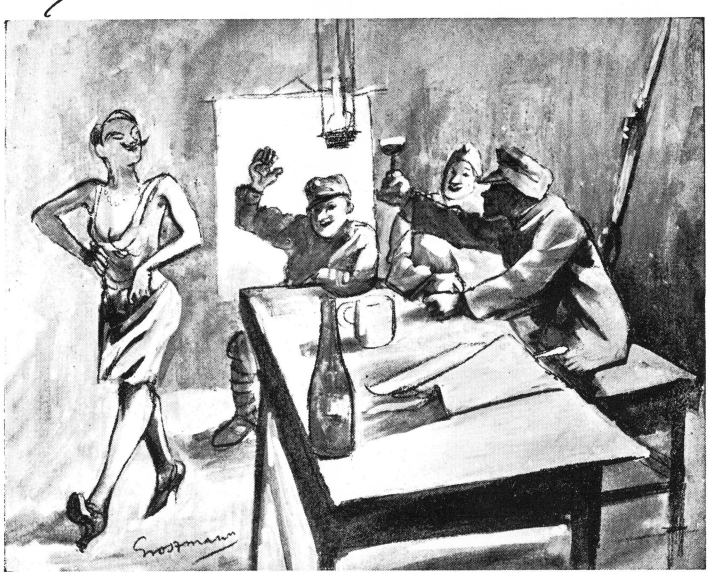

86.

The Female Warrior   1. innocence and strength

q. Who's fated to die
Alone sees my face.
Who gazes on me
Foregoes the light of his
   life.
In the heat of the fray
Heroes behold me;
Who spies my glance,
To death is doomed by my
   spear.

Brunhild, "Ring of the Nibelung"

r. The javelin and the
springboard are more
useful than lipstick...

SS Group Chief Leader
Jeckeln

Through sport to health and
   beauty.
The ideal appearance of the
   sportswoman.

Translation from the German text,
Plate 87

Durch Sport zu Gesundheit
und Schönheit.
Idealerscheinung der sportlichen Frau.
(Siebzehnjährige Deutsche.)

87.

The Female Warrior
2. innocence and strength maintained in the world of the masculine

89.

„Nun reite zu, Walküre, — Gewappnet und geschient — Der Weg, den ich dich führe, — Liegt hell und lenzbegrünt. Und steigst du erst vom Rücken — Des Rosses, goldgezäumt, Sollst du den Lorbeer pflücken, — Von dem dein Volk geträumt!"

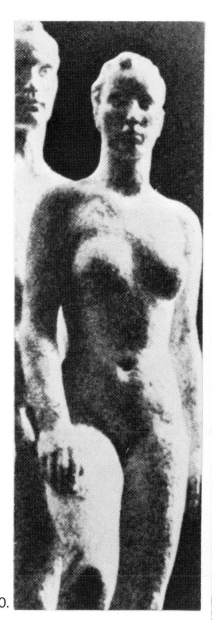

90.

S. I was stirred by the hero's holy distress;
Widely resounded the warrior's sorrow,
Free was his passion, fearful his pain,
Mournful courage, confident might;
And my ear did listen.

My eyes did look on what bade in fullness
My heart with holy fervor to beat;
Shy, astonished, stood I ashamed,
I could consider but how to serve him.

Brunhild, "Ring of the Nibelung"

Now ride forth Valkyr—
weaponed and armored—
The way that I lead you
lies bright and spring-green.
And when you descend from the
horse which is golden-harnessed,
You shall pluck the laurel of which
your people dreamed.

Translation from German text,
Plate 89

Führerinnen des weiblichen 91.
Arbeitsdienstes

92.

The Female Warrior
3. innocence and strength lost in the world of the masculine

94.

95.

Die ungarische Frontkämpferin E. K.
in feldmäßiger Ausrüstung
Nach einer photographischen Aufnahme

t. What strikes me with its gleaming?
What is this glimmering glare of steel? . . .
Shining weapons? . . .
Ha! a mail-clad man! . . .
His helmet burdens
His proud brow.
If loosened, he would rest lighter.

Ah! — how fair! . . .
This is no man!
Burning enchantment
Charges my heart; . . .
My senses wander
And waver.

Weibliche Soldaten.

Marie von Fery-Bognár, ein weiblicher Korporal.

Siegfried, "Ring of the Nibelung"

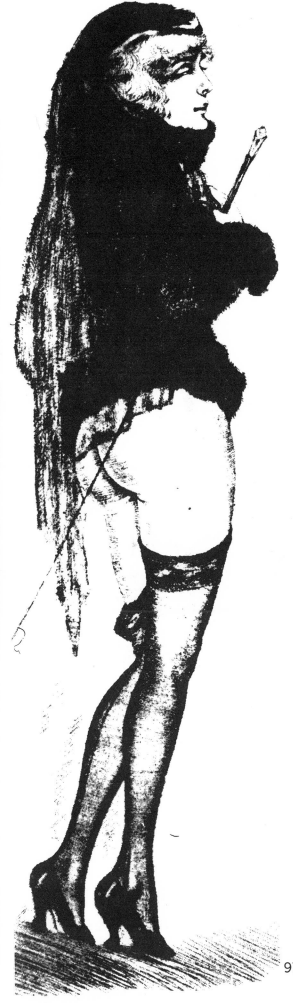

96.

97.

Karikaturistische Radierung von Max Brüning

98.

Der Sieg des Lebens.

Statistische Feststellungen ergeben einen sehr günstigen Stand unserer Säuglingswohlfahrt.

u. That was she, the tall, almost masculine woman who resembled her son, with maternal traits, severity, passion; beautiful and alluring, beautiful and unapproachable, daemon and mother, fate and beloved. There was no mistaking her!

Hermann Hesse

Archduchess Augusta of Austria as a Red Cross nurse

Through her loving behavior the archduchess has found many friends and has earned their gratefulness in the hospitals of Budapest.
From the original German text of Plate 100

The Triumph of Life

Statistical analyses gave a very favorable report on the welfare of our infants.

Translation from the German Text, plate 98

99.

100.

101.

The Iron Virgin   2. the aunt

102.

Feſt-Morgen.   Die dicke Berta gratuliert.

103.

Nach dem Balle.
Zeichnung von Heinrich Kley   104.

106.

105.

Kaiserin Auguste Viktoria.

The Maiden   1. Snow White and Rose Red

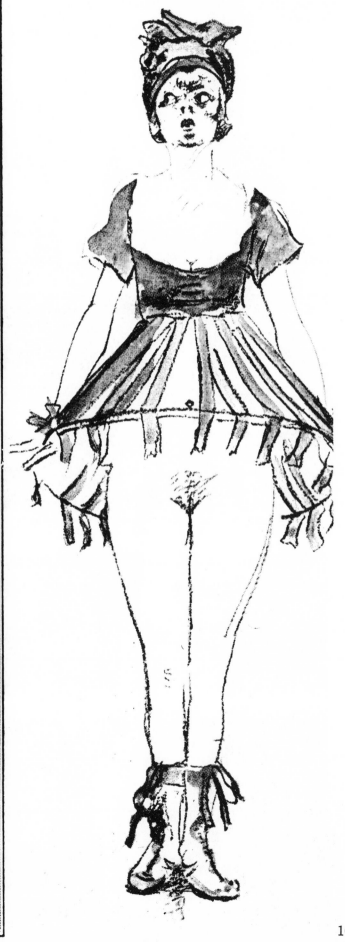

V. When our ancestors
    rode into the tour-
    nament, a wreath of
    beautiful ladies
    surrounded them
    looking down upon
    the doughty warriors.

    Wilhelm II

W. National Socialism means:
    "I do not care for the social
    issue at all. What I want is
    the folk tale."

    Thomas Mann

109.

Ausmarsch
Zeichnung von B. Wennerberg, aus »Simplicissimus«, 1915

The Maiden   1. Snow White and Rose Red

110.

Abgewiesen. Die Elsässerin: „Zieh heim, Französle, nach Bordeaux! Mei deutscher Schatz ischt wieder do,
Bei mir da glückt's dir nimmer.   Dem bleib' i treu fir immer!"

Easter

When the bells are ringing
I secretly sneak out onto
The wall and look onto the land.
Spring brings green
Shoots. Will it bring
My lover back to me?

Translation from German text,
Plate 111

Rejected

The woman from the Alsace speaks:

Go home, little Frenchy, to
    Bordeaux!
You will never succeed with me.
My German sweetheart has returned
And I'll forever be true to him.

Translation from German text, Plate 110

111. **Oſtern.**

Auf das Mäuerchen am Haus
Will ich heimlich ſteigen
Und ich ſpäh' ins Land hinaus,
Wenn die Glocken ſchweigen.

Wenn die weichen Winde weh'n
Durch die grünen Triebe,
Bringt das große Auferſtehn
Einen, den ich liebe?

Daß er, heil und glückbeſchwingt,
Fern von Grab und Gräben,
Mir erſtand'ne Freude bringt
In das junge Leben!

The Maiden   1. Snow White and Rose Red

113.

Eine moderne Venus

115.

Die Mode-Sünderin.

Michel, hab' ich dir weh getan?
So schöne Federn hatte der Hahn.
Der Hahn in friedlichen Tagen –
Er stand so stolz auf gallischem Mist,
Und ich hab', schwach wie ein Weibchen ist,
So gern bunte Federn getragen . . .

Michel, es kam eine andere Zeit!
Michel, du starrst im Eisen-Kleid
Und spielst mit blutigen Messern;
Michel, ich hab' ein Gelübde getan,
Rupf ihn gehörig, den gallischen Hahn,
Und schau's ich will mich bessern! r.

114.

Im Sonderzug nach Nürnberg

116.

Snow White and Rose Red

Once upon a time there was a widow who lived alone in a forest hut with her two children, Snow White and Rose Red. They were named after the white and red roses that grew around the cottage. Rose Red and Snow White were as happy and agreeable as any children in Germany, which as anyone knows has more happy, agreeable children than any other country in the world.

Snow White was quiet and gentle, staying home and helping her mother, while Rose Red was lively and joyful and liked to run in the forest and meadows.

They often walked hand in hand into the forest to gather berries. And no accident ever befell them, for the deer would eat out of their hands and birds would perch on their shoulders and talk to them.

One cold evening while they were returning from a walk in the forest, they met a bear standing in the path. Although they were not frightened, they were certainly startled. But the bear spoke to them and said, "I will not harm you, I only want to warm my-self for the night."

"Come in and lie down by the fire," said their mother. The bear came in that night and every night through the long winter. The children became quite friendly with him after awhile and laughingly pulled his shaggy hair and rolled him about.

When spring came, the bear said, "I must leave now to guard my treasure from the evil dwarf and will not

Der Stürmer

Deutsches Wochenblatt zum Kampfe um die Wahrheit

HERAUSGEBER JULIUS STREICHER

| Nummer 30 | Erscheint wöchentl. Einzel-Nr. 20 Pfg. Bezugspreis monatlich 54 Pfg. zuzügl. Post- u. Zustellgeld. Bestellungen bei dem Briefträger oder der zuständ. Poststelle. Nachbestellungen a. d. Verlag. Ist in der Fortsetzungsannahme 14 Tage vor Erscheinen. Preis für Geschäfts-Anzeigen: Die ca. 22 mm breite, 1 mm hohe Raum-Zeile im Anzeigenteil — .15 RM. | Nürnberg, 1 Juli 1939 | | 17. Jahr 1939 |

Juden tarnen sich!

Durchtriebene Tarnungsmethoden des Juden
Der Prozeß Homberger in Mainz / Deutsches Volk, bleib wach!

Das nationalsozialistische Deutschland hat sich zum Ziele gesetzt, das deutsche Volk von dem Einfluß fremder Völker zu entziehen und dem Einfluß fremder Völker zu entsichern. Die Kultur und Ehre des Volkes. Die Verordnungen des Reiches vom 12. November 1938 schalten den Juden aus der deutschen Wirtschaft aus.

Die Nürnberger Gesetze bestrafen die jüdischen Rassenschänder mit schweren Zuchthausstrafen. Trotzdem läßt der Jude nicht von der Rassenschande. Trotzdem macht er sich immer wieder an deutsche Frauen und Mädchen heran, um das Volk zu vergiften. Ebensowenig wie die Gesetze des denkwürdigen Reichstages zu Nürnberg den Juden veranlassen können, der Rassenschande zu entsagen, sowenig vermögen die Verordnungen des letzten Herbstes den Juden zu bestimmen, sich aus der deutschen Wirtschaft auszuschalten. Der Jude kümmert sich nicht um die Gesetze des gastgebenden Landes. Er erkennt nur jene Verordnungen an, die in seinem Gesetzbuch Talmud-Schulchan-aruch niedergelegt sind. Hier steht geschrieben:

„Der Jude darf sich nicht richten nach den Staatsgesetzen der Akum (Nichtjuden). Er hat sich zu richten nach den Gesetzen der Juden, denn sonst wären diese ja überflüssig." (Choschen ha-mischpat 368, 11 Haga.)

Aus dem Inhalt

Judenfrechheit in England
Weiße Juden auch in Wien!
Aus der Reichshauptstadt
Seidenhausjude Rudolf Weiß
So arbeiten Judenanwälte
Sie halten es mit Juden!
Semi Strauß

Im Solde Judas

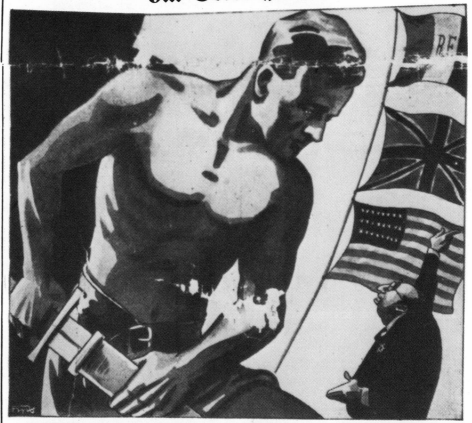

Wer sich dem Juden unterstellt
Ist Scherge nur - doch niemals Held

Und wer für Juda zieht das Schwert
Ist nie des Kampfes Lorbeer wert

Die Juden sind unser Unglück!

X. Hear you aright?
  Have Heed!
Have heed of the nightborn host,
When the Nibelung's
  hoard shall ascend
From silent depth into day!

Alberich, "Ring of the Nibelung"

Y. I'll wield the Nibelung's ring;
Then the hallowed king
Of heroes shall cower!
Valhall's heights
Storm I with Hella's host,
And rule the world by my
  will!

Alberich, "Ring of the Nibelung"

return until the fall." And so their great friendly guest left. The maidens were very sad, but bid him goodbye.

As they went into the forest one day for some sticks, they saw a dwarf with a wrinkled face and a long white beard. The end of his beard was caught in a split in a tree. "You foolish girl," he said, looking at Snow White, "why don't you get me out?" The children tried hard to pull his beard out, but it was caught too tightly. "Can't you think of anything better?" snarled the dwarf. Snow White took out her scissors and cut off the end of his beard. Snatching up his sack which was full of gold, away he went grumbling and grumping without a backward look.

Soon afterward Snow White and Rose Red found themselves again in the forest. They saw the very same dwarf near a pond. He was jumping around and was obviously in great pain, for his beard had become entangled in his fishing line. A great fish had swallowed the bait and was pulling him into the water. Snow White again pulled out her scissors and cut off another piece of his beard. "You stupid goose," said the dwarf, "you've cut off the best part of my beard." Picking up his sack of gold, he hopped over a tree stump and disappeared.

Once more the girls saw the dwarf in the woods. This time a huge eagle was trying to carry him off. The maidens ran up, caught his feet and held on until the eagle gave up. Without a word, but with an evil look, he shouldered his bag and ungratefully began to hop away. But this time their old friend the bear appeared. The dwarf turned pale yellow and through chattering teeth said to the bear, "I'm such a small morsel why don't you want these two fine plump girls?"

The bear, as he drew back his great paw, spoke and said, "Don't you recognize me little man? You are the evil dwarf who stole my gold and forced me to wander about in this forest in the guise of a bear." So saying he gave the dwarf a single blow which severed the dwarf's head from his body. Whereupon his shaggy coat disappeared and he was revealed as the king's son dressed all in gold.

The Brothers Grimm

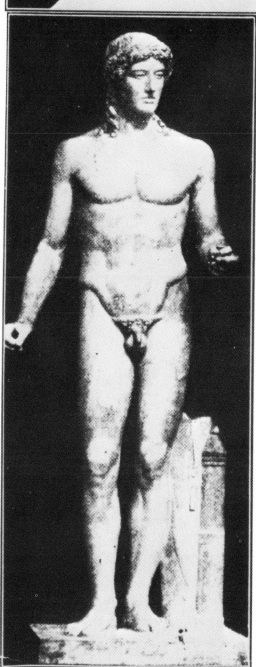

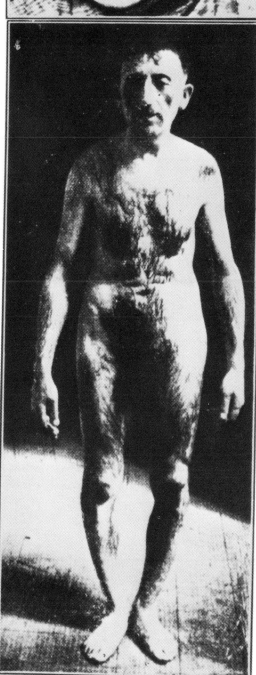

In the Pay of Judas

He who works for the Jews
Is nothing but a fake, never a hero
And he who carries the Jew's
  sword
Never gains the laurel in
  battle.

Translation from the German text,
Plate 117

Der Stürmer

Deutsches Wochenblatt zum Kampfe um die Wahrheit

HERAUSGEBER: JULIUS STREICHER

| Nummer 2 | Erscheint wöchentl. Einzel-Nr **20 Pfg.** Bezugspreis monatlich **84 Pfg.** zuzüglich Postbeſtellgeld. Beſtellungen bei dem Briefträger oder der Poſtanſtalt. Nachbeſtellungen a. d Verlag. Schluß der Anzeigenannahme 14 Tage vor Erſcheinen. Preis für Geſchäfts-Anz.: Die ca. 22 mm breite, 1 mm hohe Raum-Zeile im Anzeigenteil –.75 RM. | Nürnberg, im Januar 1938 | Der Verlag: Der Stürmer G. m. b. H. Streicher Nürnberg-A Pfarrenſtr. | 16. Jahr 1938 |

Der Handelsjude

Er schädigt das Volk und verdirbt den Kaufmannstand

Was der Talmud über den Handel sagt

Eine typiſche Erſcheinung in aller Welt iſt der jüdiſche Händler. Wohin man kommt, iſt er vertreten. Er iſt zu finden in allen Erdteilen, in allen Ländern, in allen Hafenſtädten, an allen Handelsplätzen, an allen Börſen und auf allen Märkten. Er handelt mit allem. Mit Kriegsmaterial, mit Lebensmitteln, mit Holz, mit Eiſen. Er handelt mit Rohſtoffen und mit Fertigwaren. Er handelt auch mit Menſchen. Der Jude war der Sklavenhändler der Vergangenheit. Er iſt heute der internationale Mädchenhändler.

Warum treibt der Jude mit Vorliebe den Handel? Der Jude hat nicht den Trieb zur Arbeit im Blut. Er iſt nicht dazu geboren. Er haßt die Arbeit. In ſeinem Geheimgeſetzbuch, im Talmud, ſteht geſchrieben:

"Es übt weder das wilde Tier, noch der Vogel irgend ein Handwerk aus. Darum ſoll ſich auch der Jude ohne Mühe und Arbeit ernähren." (Luiddu-ſin, Seite 82b.)

Das tut der Jude. Er ernährt ſich ohne Mühe und Arbeit. Er ſpekuliert, er ſchachert, er betrügt, er ſchwindelt, er ſchiebt, er lügt, aber er arbeitet nicht. Und er bringt überall Schaden, wo er auftritt. Er ſchadet auch dem Handel. Er ſchadet ihm in verheerender Weiſe.

Der Handel iſt keine unnütze Tätigkeit. Ohne den Handel wäre die ungeheure Entwicklung nicht denkbar, die die Völker genommen haben. Der Handel iſt das Bindeglied zwiſchen Erzeuger und Verbraucher. Zwiſchen den Rohſtoffquellen und der Fabrikation. Er befördert Güter und Material von Land zu Land. Er iſt ein wichtiger und unentbehrlicher Teil der Wirtſchaft. Der Handel nützt der Wirtſchaft. Solange der Nichtjude den

Judenrechnung

Was nützt mancher Frau ſchon das bißchen Gewiſſen
Wir ſind eben Juden, wir ſind geriſſen,
Und iſt mal eine vom Flimmer betört,
Der Judenname ſie auch nicht mehr ſtört

Aus dem Inhalt

Die Juden sind unser Unglück!

120.

122.

Der Gott der Juden

**Der Gott, der Wechsel platzen ließ
Und Völker ins Verderben stieß,
Wird trotz des Betens nicht lebendig.
Des Geldes Macht ist unbeständig**

The God of the Jews

The God who could kill credit
And push people to the edge
Cannot become alive, even with a
    prayer.
The power of money has a limit!

Translation from German text, Plate 122

Michel . . . .

Nachdruck verboten!

Zeitgesch. Sammlg. A. Wolf, Leipzig

Drastischer Hinweis auf die jüdische Vorherrschaft

121.

Z. Not till Wagner's operas
did these legends become
familiar to the mass of
ordinary Germans.
Wagner it was who almost
singlehanded steeped all
Germany in the tales of
Siegfried, his wonderful
sword, the horrible
capitalistic dragon, the
not quite Aryan little
dwarfs with their hoard
of corrupting gold.

Peter Viereck

aa. The warring German
Siegfried received a
stealthy stab in the
back.

Adolf Hitler

Geborenes Verbrechertum

Eine Judenfamilie bereitet sich für das Fest Yom Kippur in der Synagoge vor. Die Schlechtigkeit schaut schon den Jüngsten aus den Augen

Born Criminals

A Jewish family prepares itself for Yom Kippur. A criminality is already visible in the eyes of the youngest.

Translation from German text, Plate 123

Jewish Murder Feast

Each year in spring the Jews celebrate all over the world the Passover holiday—to celebrate the memory of the Jewish murder night in Egypt: the thievery of gold and silver and the migration of the children of Israel out of Egypt.

Translation from the German text, Plate 124

Foreign People, Foreign Customs

As the Jews celebrate their biggest holiday, they sit around a richly laden table with wine, fruit, and cookies and keep their hats on. When the alcohol has accomplished its effects, then they curse non-Jews and say their hate prayers.

Translation from German text, Plate 125

124.

(Das Bild erschien in der New Yorker jüdischen Zeitschrift „Forward", Ausgabe vom 2. April 1937.)

Jüdisches Mordfest

Jedes Jahr im Frühling feiern die Juden auf der ganzen Welt das Passahfest zum Andenken an die jüdische Mordnacht in Ägypten, an die jüdischen Gold- und Silberdiebstähle und an den Auszug der „Kinder Israels" aus Ägypten

Fremdes Volk, fremde Sitten

Wenn die Juden ihre höchsten Feste feiern, dann setzen sie sich, den Hut auf dem Kopfe behaltend, um einen mit Wein, Früchten und Gebäck reichbeladenen Tisch. Hat der Alkohol seine Wirkung getan, dann stoßen sie üble Verwünschungen auf die Nichtjuden aus und verrichten ihre Haßgebete.

125.

The Domestic Warrior   1. the grandfather

126.

bb. One day the Führer came out once again and greeted the people in a very friendly way. They were all full of joy and jubilation and reached out with their hands to him.
In the very first rank stood a little girl with flowers in her hands, and she said in her clear child's voice: "Today is my birthday." Thereupon the Führer took the little blond girl by the hand and walked slowly with her through the fence and into the villa. Here the little girl was treated to cake and strawberries with thick, sweet cream. And the little one ate and ate until she could eat no more. Then she said very politely: "I thank you very much!" and "Goodbye." Then she made herself as tall as she could, put her little arms around the Führer's neck, and now the little girl gave the great Führer a long, long kiss.

Wilhelm Brinkman and Paul Rossing, eds., "Fibel fur die Grundschule, im Bezirk Dusseldorf"

127.

128.

Umschlag der am 19. Januar erschei-
nenden Sondernummer der Eleganten Welt.

The Domestic Warrior   1. the grandfather

130.

132.

131.

133.

Karl der Große,
der Erneuerer des römischen und
Ahnherr des altdeutschen Kaisertums
(von Albrecht Dürer)

The Domestic Warrior   1. the grandfather

134.

135.

Silberne Medaille zur Erinnerung an die Befreiung Ostpreußens durch den Marschall v. Hindenburg.

1. The kettledrummer, during a parade at one of the Nuremberg rallies.
2. New Year's card, for the year that was to begin with the official peace conference ending World War One. The German at the top and bottom of this card reads: "A place in the sun / To anyone who does not begrudge me one." The wording echoes almost exactly remarks made earlier by Wilhelm II when he committed Germany to an expanded navy and a colonial empire at the turn of the century. Artist: Ludwig Hesshaimer.
3. The farmer and the factory.
4. Turbine factory of AEG (German General Electrical Company), Berlin, 1901. Architect: Peter Behrens. Behrens' style here and in his administrative building for the Mannesmann Works (see Plate 6) is characteristic of much of the "new" architecture that appeared in Germany after 1900. This architecture was a monument to the possibilities of the new German technology, employing new structural concepts and new materials. Although to some degree classical and traditional, these buildings bent space, molded forms and created optical illusions that made their basic geometrical patterns seem plastic and fluid. The work of Poelzig (Plate 5), of Bonatz (Plate 8), Fischer (Plates 26 and 31) and Dülfer (Plate 35) is comparable to the work of Behrens, and all are considered to be part of what is known as the German Expressionist tradition. Although the work of these architects was radical and liberal and laid the groundwork for the Bauhaus movement, which was strongly anti-Nazi, these architects also influenced Nazi architecture, which had a similar blend of classicism and plasticity. Compare the structures of Troost (Plate 30), Speer (Plates 7, 34 and 67) and Klotz (Plate 10).
5. Water tower. Architect: Hans Poelzig. See note to Plate 4.
6. Administration building of the Mannesmann Works. Architect: Peter Behrens. See note to Plate 4.
7. Entrance to Convention Hall, Luipold Arena, Nuremberg, 1935. Architect: Albert Speer. Speer was considered by the Nazis to be the master builder for the new Germany. He was especially adept at designing public buildings that impressively framed large numbers of participants in elaborate and dramatic tableaux. In addition to Convention Hall, he designed the Zeppelinfeld at Nuremberg (Plate 34), a complex of buildings and arenas used as the backdrop for the annual party congresses. Working directly under Hitler, in 1937 he started to remodel Berlin; and in 1938, he designed the Reich Chancellery (Plate 67).
8. Canal works on Neckar River, 1926. Architect: Paul Bonatz. See note to Plate 4.
9. Tank of government troops in the Siegesalle, Berlin, 1919.
10. Ordensburg Vogelsang, ca. 1933. Architect: Clemens Klotz. This was one of several military or leadership schools the Nazis constructed. All were deliberate attempts to reconstruct the style and environment of medieval German castles and fortresses, yet they used a nonornamented line similar to that in the work of Behrens (see Plate 4). The German caption reads: "At Ordensburg, the party's second generation of leaders becomes welded together."
11. Section of Plate 3.
12. Repeat of Plate 2.
13. The remains of fortifications from World War One.
14. Marksburg Castle on the Rhine. Architect: Bodo Ebhardt. This was one of many structures built at the turn of the century that attempted to duplicate the style of the original Rhine castles. The intent was to shape the twentieth-century landscape. By re-creating a medieval environment, architects like Ebhardt believed they could also re-create the medieval traditions and patterns of behavior that went with that environment. (For an example of a memorial constructed in the same period and with the same purpose, see Plate 39.)
15. "Rejected!" Artist: Lutz Ehrenberger. *Kriegs-Nummer 89*, 1916.
16. "Easter." A portion of the German verse is translated above Plate 111. Artist: Ernst Heilemann. *Kriegs-Nummer 90*, 1916.
17. Mobile bordello for officers, World War One.
18. Section of a relief, *The Peasants: Commerce and Trade*, Leipzig, 1928. Architect: German Bestelmeyer.
19. Section of Plate 3.
20. New Year's card, 1916, in which the New Year, pictured as a child, greets a couple at the gates of his home. Artist: Rudolf Schiestl.
21. A housing project built after World War One to recapture the forms of peasant life. Architect: Paul Wolf.
22. Mural above the entrance to the post office, Kochel. Artist: Demmel.
23. The Wählburg, considered to be "the most beautiful German farmhouse."
24. Tent constructed during a Nuremberg rally to imitate style of a typical German farmhouse.
25. Farmer plowing beside autobahn. The original caption for this picture remarked that the autobahn exactly parallels the route of an old Roman aqueduct and calls the new German highway "The Road of Leaders." In the middle of the picture, between the farmer and the highway, is a column from the earlier Roman structure.
26. Detail of a school. Architect: Theodor Fischer. See note to Plate 4.
27. Repeat of Plate 2.
28. Mobile chapel car, World War One.
29. Recruiting poster, World War One.
30. House of German Art, Munich, begun in 1933. Architect: Paul Ludwig Troost. Troost was Hitler's first important architect. Hitler was so involved in Troost's architectural plans that Nazi literature claimed that he was codesigner of this building.
31. Garrison Church. Architect: Theodor Fischer. See note to Plate 4.
32. War Memorial Church in New-Ulm, 1923. Architect: Dominikus Böhm. Böhm was a student of Theodor Fischer.
33. Watchtower constructed for a Nuremberg rally.
34. Zeppelinfeld, Nuremberg, 1934–1936. Architect: Albert Speer. See note to Plate 7.
35. Theater. Architect: Martin Dülfer. See note to Plate 4.
36. Memorial at General Headquarters, Munich. The plaque in the background commemorates the dead of November 9, 1923. Hitler dedicated *Mein Kampf* to them, claiming them as the first martyrs of the Third Reich. The slate carries the inscription: "And you have indeed conquered."
37. Naval War Memorial, Laboe at the Kieler Ford. Architect: G. A. Munzer. A brick tower, erected in 1930, it was constructed to look like a ship's prow about to be launched.
38. A war memorial to riflemen, constructed soon after World War One. The inscription at the base is: "We were united in love for the homeland / And have given her [our] all. / Brother—How little is your striving."
39. People's Memorial to the Slain, Leipzig, begun 1900. Architect: Bruno Schmitz. The construction of memorials and monuments in Germany was inspired by the general feeling that the year 1900 marked the end of an old era and the beginning of a new one. This was greeted with as much misgiving as joy. After World War One, the construction of monuments was stimulated by a spirit of rebirth and rededication; and the monuments built after the war, in the late 20s and early 30s, were more deliberately stark and aggressive. With the rise of the Nazis, monuments were built to memorialize the new German heroes of the Third Reich (Plate 36) as well as to connect the history of the Third Reich to the history of earlier German victories and defeats (Plates 40, 57 and 58).

40. The Tannenberg Monument. Architects: Walter and Johannes Kruger. Built in 1927 as a memorial to the freeing of East Prussia, it is explicitly a walled fortress. When Hindenburg died, he was buried there by Hitler, and the monument was renamed "The Reich War Memorial."

41. Statue of Otto the Great. The caption explains that Otto the Great was "the first to wear the crown of the old German Reich."

42. Third encampment of the Hitler youth, Weimar.

43. Luftwaffe and swastika.

44. Parade of panzer tanks.

45. *Work Corps*, a painting. Artist: Ferdinand Staeger.

46. Section of Plate 1.

47. Kaiser Wilhelm II. Artist: Ernst Heilemann. *Kriegs-Nummer 8*, 1914.

48. Repeat of Plate 47, complete cover. A translation of the caption at the bottom is: "Until they [the enemy] lie bowed to the ground, lead your troops from victory to victory, thinking about your brave forebears."

49. Hitler in 1923.

50. Kaiser Wilhelm II as supreme commander-in-chief.

51. *Caisse*, wood cut. Artist: Franz Masereel.

52. Field Marshal Helmuth von Moltke, the chief military strategist for Prussia in the war against Austria (1866) and the war against France (1870).

53. A member of the Work Corps saluting.

54. "Encouragement," a poem. Poet: Rudolf Presber, editor of *Lustige Blätter*. *Kriegs-Nummer 14*, 1914.

55. Repeat of Plate 29, complete poster. The German slogan says: "Protect your Homeland! Enlist in the Free Corps."

56. "The submarine service: 'Ready! Fire!'" Artist: W. A. Wellner. *Kriegs-Nummer 132*, 1917.

57. Mosaic in memorial hallway, Adolf Hitler Passwalk. Artist: Georg Gruber.

58. Military Service, memorial to the fallen of World War One, Munich. Sculptor: Bernhard Bleeker.

59. *Youth Service*, statue of Hitler Youth. Sculptor: Bernhard Lohf.

60. SS soldier on guard.

61. Hitler youth on honor guard.

62. War-loan poster. The German slogan says: "Help us win! Support the war loan." *Kriegs-Nummer 141*, 1917.

63. *Man and Woman*, a statue. Sculptor: Georg Kolbe. Kolbe was an important German sculptor in the 20s and through the Nazi period. He was not, strictly speaking, a Nazi sculptor, although his work was much appreciated and well rewarded by them.

64. *Prince Eugene*, a painting. Eugene was an Austrian general instrumental in defeating the French at Blenheim (1704). This painting, along with pictures of Moltke (Plate 52), Schiller and Fredrick the Great, is used as an example of the ideal German form in Christoffel's *Volk—Bewegung—Reich*.

65. *Perseus and Andromeda*. Artist: Louis Corinth, 1901.

66. *Bamberg Rider*, thought to be a thirteenth-century statue of Conrad III. This statue was one of the most popular works of traditional art in the Nazi period, appearing over and over again in various publications and contexts as the ideal image of a kaiser.

67. Torchbearer, entitled *Partei*, in front of the Reich Chancellery, Berlin. Sculptor: Arno Breker. Architect: Albert Speer. See note to Plate 7. Breker was the Nazis' most important sculptor; his work was considered the fulfillment of Nazi theory in form.

68. "The Fashion Sinner." Artist: Bayros. *Kriegs-Nummer 94*, 1916.

69. Wilhelm, crown prince of the German Reich and of Prussia, commander-in-chief of the Fifth Army.

70. A typical German officer in field uniform, home from the front.

71. Section of Plate 68.

72. "Children of War." Artist: Ernst Heilemann. *Kriegs-Nummer 99*, 1916.

73. "The Crown Prince." Artist: Ernst Heilemann. *Kriegs-Nummer 5*, 1914.

74. Friedrich Wilhelm von Seydlitz, a general who served under Fredrick the Great.

75. Repeat of Plate 72, complete.

76. Cartoon, "The Mishandling of Little Girls at the Workhouse." A rough translation of the rest of the caption reads: "A picture of youth—sensational proceedings."

77. "In Front of the Palace." Poet: Oscar Blumenthal. *Kriegs-Nummer 9*, 1914.

78. Cartoon, "What Is the German Fatherland?" Represented in this cartoon are the external enemies of Germany, in particular the French, who had taken advantage of Germany's division into independent states (among them, Hesse, Baden, Wurtemberg, Saxony, Bavaria and Prussia). "Plon-Plon"—the nickname of Prince Napoleon Bonaparte, cousin to Napoleon III and leader of the Bonapartist party in the 1880s—stands for Napoleonic imperialism. Frossard was a general of the French forces that invaded Germany during the Franco-Prussian War. Mc-Mahon, also an invading general during the Franco-Prussian War, was president of the French Republic in the 1870s. And the three figures to the right of the cartoon (*Es, Sie* and *Er* or "it, she and he") portray other German enemies, those who have been and those yet to come.

79. "On Command."

80. "The Stinkroom." Originally in a military newspaper, *An Flanderns Küste* (1915), a rough translation of the German verse is: "The stinkroom is the gas mask's final proof— / It's for fops to pump water under the roof. / Here, wild, snouted creatures grunt for their air. / Against outhouses, what can compare?"

81. "An Adventure at the Seat of War, World War One."

82. Instructions on the use of the field latrine.

83. "The March on Paris." Described as "a political-erotic picture by a German soldier: the Paris he conceives while in the trenches."

84. Homosexuals, a group portrait.

85. "In Drag." Artist: L. Grossmann.

86. "Imitations in the barracks." Artist: L. Grossmann.

87. "Through Sport to Health and Beauty."

88. *Germania in Power*. Artist: F. A. von Kaulbach.

89. Hindenburg and the Valkyr. Hindenburg is speaking to the Valkyr, who represents Germany, as in Plate 88. After his victory over the Russian armies in East Prussia early in World War One, Hindenburg became in the German mind the archetype for the complete soldier-statesman (see Plates 102, 129 and 134). Toward the end of the war, he was made chief of staff of the army. And finally in the last days of the Weimar Republic, still standing for stability and the old imperial style, he became Germany's head of state. Understanding Hindenburg's symbolic value, Hitler worked through him to gain power legally in 1933. Artist: W. A. Wellner. *Kriegs-Nummer 87*, 1916.

90. *Boy and Girl*, a statue. Sculptor: Georg Kolbe. See note to Plate 63.

91. Salute from members of the Women's Work Corps.

92. "We lead in the contest for young ladies!"

93. A lady corporal.

94. Female soldiers.

95. "A front-line fighter." The caption explains that this is "a Hungarian woman, in field pack, who received the German Iron Cross."

96. A female cadet candidate.

97. Caricature. Artist: Max Brüning.

98. "The Triumph of Life." Artist: F. Jüttner. *Kriegs-Nummer 149*, 1917.

99. *Fullness of Youth*, "Motherly Type of Woman." Artist: Paul Herrmann.

100. Archduchess Augusta of Austria.

101. *Maternal Joy of the Working Class.* Artist: Karl Oscar Piszte.
102. "Happy Day. Congratulations from Big Bertha." See note to Plate 89. *Kriegs-Nummer 89,* 1916.
103. "The Big Bertha." *Kriegs-Nummer 89,* 1916.
104. "After the Ball." Artist: Heinrich Kley.
105. Empress Auguste Viktoria, the wife of Wilhelm II.
106. "A letter from home by Anna, the cook, to her boyfriend on the front." From an advertisement for a magazine called *Knapsack Humor,* in *Kriegs-Nummer 82,* 1916.
107. *Flora.* Artist: Benedict Masson.
108. The dancer Anita Berber, popular in the 1920s. Artist: Charlotte Berend.
109. "Departure." Artist: B. Wennerberg.
110. Repeat of Plate 15, complete.
111. Repeat of Plate 16.
112. "The Rendezvous." The verse on this postcard says: "I know a quiet corner, / In intimate secrecy, / There I and my true love / Are always safe."
113. "A modern Venus," the film actress, Iwa Wanja.
114. Special train to Nuremberg.
115. Repeat of Plate 68.
116. Section of Plate 65.
117. Front page of *Der Stürmer,* July, 1939. The motto for the masthead of *Der Stürmer* was: "The German paper alert to the struggle for truth." Edited by Julius Streicher, a close friend of Hitler, *Der Stürmer* filled its pages with perhaps the most obscene anti-Semitism ever printed. The headline for this issue is: "Jews Camouflage Themselves." The rallying call for the newspaper, which appeared regularly at the bottom, was: "The Jews are our misfortune!"
118. A racial comparison. *Der Stürmer,* January 7, 1943.
119. Front page of *Der Stürmer,* January, 1938. The headline reads: "The Jewish Merchant—he cheats the people and destroys the good name of honest merchants." The caption over the picture is: "Jewish Calculations." A free translation of the doggerel verse under the picture is: "What happens to a woman's conscience? / How easily tainted—like a Jew— / By bits of glitter quickly seduced. / The Jewish stain blithely reduced."
120. "Hiding the Gold," an illustration in a serialized story, *The Rhinish Rebel, A Story of Bygone Days.* Chapter VI, where this illustration occurs, is called "Jewish Terror on the Rhine." *Der Stürmer,* April 24, 1941.
121. Cartoon, "Word to the Wise: the Jewish order of things." Michael is a traditional figure for Germany; often he is pictured as a knight.
122. Cartoon, "The God of the Jews." *Der Stürmer,* May 29, 1941.
123. "Born Criminals." *Der Stürmer,* May 15, 1941.
124. "Jewish Murder Feast." This rather innocuous picture was originally printed in *Forward* (April 28, 1940), a magazine published in New York. It was the habit of *Der Stürmer* to take pictures like this one from American periodicals, add appropriate captions and then use them as documentation for their racial theories. Reprinted in *Der Stürmer,* May 1, 1941.
125. "Foreign People, Foreign Customs." *Der Stürmer,* June 10, 1943.
126. Hitler, a little girl and a baby carriage.
127. Hitler at an East Prussian farmhouse.
128. The cover of the magazine *Elegante Welt,* January 19, 1916. From an advertisement in *Kriegs-Nummer 77,* 1916.
129. Hindenburg. See note to Plate 89. Artist: Ernst Heilemann. The cover of *Kriegs-Nummer 87,* 1916.
130. Inspector general of the German army, World War One, Ritter von Auffenberg.
131. Bismarck, ca. 1894.
132. New Year's card from a brewery, 1918. Artist: Hans Röhm.
133. Karl the Great (Charlemagne). As the caption explains, he was considered to be "the restorer of the Romans and the founding father of the old German Empire."
134. Top coin, enlarged, with image of Hindenburg killing Russian bear, and coin to far right: obverse and reverse of medal commemorating the liberation of East Prussia from the Russians, 1914. See note to Plate 89.
135. Two coins from the left: obverse and reverse of medal in honor of Archduke Frederick of Austria. The inscription on the reverse side says: "Soldiers! Through your incomparable valor you have received the highest military honor."

Appendix 2. Sources for Visual and Written Material

Authors' collection. Plate 61 and Captions m and v.

Authors' version. "Rose White and Rose Red."

Binding, Rudolf Georg. *Vom Leben der Plastik: Inhalt und Schönheit des Werkes von Georg Kolbe.* Berlin: Rembrandt-Verlag, 1932. Plate 90.

Bonatz (Paul): Arbeiten aus den Jahren 1907 bis 1937. Ed. Friedrich Tamms. Stuttgart: Julius Hoffmann, 1937. Plate 8.

Braungart, Richard. *Neue deutsche Gelegenheits-graphik.* Munich: F. Hanfstaengl, 1921. Plates 2, 12, 20, 27 and 132.

Burke, Kenneth. *A Grammar of Motives and a Rhetoric of Motives.* Berkeley, Cal.: University of California Press, 1969. Reprinted by permission of Mr. Burke. Captions c, e and j.

Christoffel, Karl. *Volk—Bewegung—Reich.* Frankfurt (Main): M. Diesterweg, 1944. Plates 23, 30, 41, 45, 52, 58, 59, 64, 66 and 133.

Decker, Will. *Kreuze am Wege zur Freiheit.* Leipzig: Koehler & Amelang, 1935. Plates 9, 37, 38 and 40.

Edelman, Murray. *The Symbolic Uses of Politics.* Urbana, Ill.: University of Illinois Press, 1967. Reprinted by permission of the publishers. Captions a, h and i.

Frohes Schaffen: Ein Haus Buch deutscher Jugend. Eds. Karl Springenschmid and Anton Hadwiger. Leipzig: Deutscher Verlag für Jugend und Volk, 1938–1943. Publication began in 1924? Subtitle varies; from 1939, *Das Jahrbuch der deutschen Jugend der Ostmark.* Plates 13 (XVI), 25 (XVI) and 53 (XVI).

Fuchs, Eduard. *Die Karikatur der europäischen Völker vom Jahre 1848 bis zur Gegenwart.* Berlin: A. Hofmann & Co., 1906. Plate 78.

Gauss, Christian. *The German Emperor as Shown in His Public Utterances.* New York: Scribner's, 1915. Reprinted by permission of the publishers. Captions b and l.

Helmolt, Hans Ferdinand. *Der Weltkrieg in Bildern und Dokumenten.* 4 vols. Leipzig: Johannes M. Meulenhoff, 1914–1917. Plates 50 (I), 69 (I), 70 (I), 93 (III), 100 (III), 105 (I), 130 (I), 134 (II), and 135 (III).

Hesse, Hermann. *Demian.* New York: Harper & Row, 1965. Reprinted by permission of English publishers, Vision Press and Peter Owen. Caption u.

Historisches Bildarchiv Handke, Bad Berneck, Germany. Plate 131.

Hitler, Adolf. *Mein Kampf.* Trans. John Chamberlain *et al.* New York: Reynal & Hitchcock, 1939. Reprinted by permission of Harcourt, Brace & World. Caption aa.

Hoffmann, Heinrich. *Jugend um Hitler: 120 Bilddokumente aus der Umgebung des Führers.* Munich: Heinrich Hoffmann Verlag, 1943. Plates 126 and 127.

Jungen—eure Welt! Das Jahrbuch der Hitler-Jugend. Eds. Karl Lapper and Wilhelm Utermann. Munich: F. Eher

Nachf. (Zentralverlag der NSDAP), 1938–1943. Editors and subtitle vary. Plates 42 (II), 74 (III) and 92 (II).

Kolbe, Georg. *Werke der Letzten Jahre*. Introd. Wilhelm Pinder. Berlin: Rembrandt-Verlag, 1937. Reprinted by permission of the publisher. Plate 63.

Kriegs-Album der Lustigen Blätter. 7 vols. Berlin: Eysler & Co. (Verlag der Lustigen Blätter), 1914–1917. Plates 15 (IV), 16 (IV), 47 (I), 48 (I), 54 (I), 56 (VI), 62 (VI), 68 (IV), 71 (IV), 72 (IV), 73 (I), 75 (IV), 77 (I), 89 (IV), 98 (VI), 102 (IV), 103 (IV), 106 (IV), 110 (IV), 111 (IV), 115 (IV), 128 (IV) and 129 (IV).

Kulturgeschichte. First of 4 vols.: *Bilder-Lexikon*. Vienna: Verlag für Kulturforschung, 1928. Plates 76 and 97.

Kunst und Kunsthandwerk am Bau. Stuttgart: Julius Hoffmann, 1937. Plates 18 and 22.

Mead, George H. *Mind, Self and Society*. Chicago: University of Chicago Press, 1934. Copyright © 1934 by University of Chicago. Reprinted by permission of the publishers. Caption f.

Moreck, Curt. *Kultur-und Sittengeschichte der Neuesten Zeit*. Dresden: Paul Aretz, 1928. Plates 51, 65, 99, 101, 104, 107, 108, 113 and 116.

Mosse, George L., ed. *Nazi Culture*. New York: Grosset & Dunlap, 1966. Copyright © 1966 by George L. Mosse. Reprinted by permission of the publishers. Captions g, r and bb.

Nationalsozialistische Deutsche Arbeiterpartei. *Ich Kämpfe*. Munich: F. Eher Nachf., 1943. Plates 3, 10, 11, 19, 34, 36, 57, 60 and 67.

———. *Reichstagung in Nürnberg, 1933–1938*. 6 vols. Vols. 1 and 2, ed. Julius Streicher; Vols. 3 through 6, ed. Hanns Kerrl. Berlin: C. A. Weller, 1933–1939. Plates 1 (1935), 7 (1936), 24 (1936), 33 (1937), 43 (1935), 44 (1936), 46 (1935), 91 (1936) and 114 (1936).

Pirandello, Luigi. *Henry IV*, from *Naked Masks: Five Plays*. Ed. Eric Bentley. Trans. Edward Storer. Copyright © 1922 and 1952 by E. P. Dutton & Company, Inc., New York. Renewal 1950, in the names of Stefano, Fausto and Lietta Pirandello. Reprinted by permission of E. P. Dutton and International Copyright Bureau, Ltd. The quotation from the title page.

Schumacher, Fritz. *Strömungen in deutscher Baukunst seit 1800*. Leipzig: E. A. Seemann, 1935. Plates 4, 5, 6, 14, 21, 26, 31, 32, 35 and 39.

Sittengeschichte des Weltkriegs, I. Ed. Magnus Hirschfeld. Leipzig: Schneider & Co., 1930. Plates 17, 79, 80, 81, 82, 83, 84, 85, 86, 87, 94, 95, 96, 109 and 112.

Stern, Fritz. *The Politics of Cultural Despair: A Study in the Rise of the Germanic Ideology*. Berkeley, Cal.: University of California Press, 1961. Reprinted by permission of The Regents of the University of California. Captions k, n, o and p.

Der Stürmer. Ed. Julius Streicher. Nuremberg: 1922?–1945? (Files for this newspaper are generally incomplete; we have used the collection in The Center for Research Libraries, Chicago, Ill., which is reasonably full for the war years, especially 1941–1944.) Plates 117, 118, 119, 120, 122, 123, 124 and 125.

Usadel, Georg. *Zeitgeschichte in Wort und Bild, 1918–1920*. Oldenburg: Kultur & Aufbau Verlags, 1937. Plates 29, 49, 55 and 121.

Viereck, Peter. *Meta-Politics: The Roots of the Nazi Mind*. New York: Putnam's, 1965. Copyright © 1941 by Alfred A. Knopf, Inc. Renewal 1961 and 1965 by Peter Viereck. Reprinted by permission of the publishers. Captions w and z.

Wagner, Richard. *Authentic Libretti of the Wagner Operas*. New York: Crown Publishers, 1938. Copyright © 1938, 1966. Reprinted by permission of the publishers. Caption s.

Wagner, Richard. *Poems: The Ring of the Nibelung*. Rev. ed. Trans. and ed. George T. Dippold. New York: Henry Holt and Company, 1888. Captions d, q, t, x and y.

Der Weltkrieg Illustrierte. 10 vols. Leipzig: Velhagen & Klasing, 1915–1919. Plates 28 (II) and 88 (VI).

Appendix 3. Readings

Given the experimental nature of this book, we have used the following list not only to indicate our specific indebtedness but also to suggest related approaches in fields and disciplines only indirectly connected to the period of German history under study but central to the method of this book. We hope that this latter category of books will be helpful to readers interested in pursuing some of the methodological issues raised by this study; books in this category roughly range in that area created by the tangencies of sociology, psychology, aesthetics and the structural analysis of culture.

Discussions of Art and Architecture and Supplementary Visual Sources

Chicago, Art Institute. *Exhibition of Contemporary German Art, 1909*. Berlin: G. Stilke, 1908.

Helmolt, Hans Ferdinand. *Bismarck, der eisern Kanzler: Zugleich Bismarcks Leben in Bildern und Dockumenten*. Leipzig: Johannes M. Meulenhoff, 1915.

Lane, Barbara M. *Architecture and Politics in Germany, 1918–1945*. Cambridge: Harvard University Press, 1968.

Lehmann-Haupt, Hellmut. *Art under a Dictatorship*. New York: Oxford University Press, 1954.

A Nation Builds: Contemporary German Architecture. Ed. German Library of Information. New York: German Library of Information, 1940.

Platz, Gustav Adolf. *Die Baukunst der Neuesten Zeit*. Berlin: Propyläen, 1927.

Stein, Walther. *Bismarck: Des eisernen Kanslers Leben in annaherd 200 Bildern*. Siegen: Hermann Montanus, 1915.

Wolters, Rudolf. *Albert Speer*. Oldenburg: Gerhard Stalling, 1943.

Das Zeitalter des Imperialismus, 1890–1930. Propyläen-Weltgeschichte, vol. 10. Berlin: Propyläen, 1933.

German Ideology

Kohn, Hans. *The Mind of Germany*. New York: Harper & Row, 1965.

Mosse, George L. *The Crisis of German Ideology: Intellectual Origins of the Third Reich*. New York: Grosset & Dunlap, 1964.

Santayana, George. *The German Mind: A Philosophical Diagnosis*. New York: Thomas Y. Crowell Company, 1968.

Stern, Fritz. *The Politics of Cultural Despair: A Study in the Rise of the Germanic Ideology*. Berkeley, Cal.: University of California Press, 1961.

Viereck, Peter. *Meta-Politics: The Roots of the Nazi Mind*. New York: Putnam's, 1965.

Von Klemperer, Klemens. *Germany's New Conservatism: Its History and Dilemma in the Twentieth Century*. Princeton, N.J.: Princeton University Press, 1968.

German History

Ashley, Annie. *The Social Policy of Bismarck*. London: Longmans, Green and Company, 1912.

Balfour, Michael. *The Kaiser and His Times*. Boston: Houghton Mifflin, 1964.

Barnett, Correlli. *The Swordbearers: Supreme Command in the First World War.* New York: New American Library, 1965.

Barraclough, G. *The Origins of Modern Germany.* Rev. ed. New York: Putnam's, 1963.

Bramsted, Ernest K. *Goebbels and National Socialist Propaganda, 1925–1945.* East Lansing, Michigan: Michigan State University Press, 1965.

Craig, Gordon A. *From Bismarck to Adenauer: Aspects of German Statecraft.* Rev. ed. New York: Harper & Row, 1965.

Grunberger, Richard. *Germany: 1918–1945.* New York: Harper & Row, 1967.

Hart, B. H. Liddell. *The German Generals Talk.* New York: William Morrow and Company, 1948.

Jarman, T. L. *The Rise and Fall of Nazi Germany.* New York: New American Library, 1961.

Medlicott, W. N. *Bismarck and Modern Germany.* New York: Harper & Row, 1965.

Nowak, Karl Friedrich. *Kaiser and Chancellor.* Trans. E. W. Dickes. New York: Macmillan, 1930.

Rosenberg, Arthur. *The Birth of the German Republic, 1871–1918.* Trans. Ian F. D. Morrow. London: Oxford University Press, 1931.

Shirer, William L. *The Rise and Fall of the Third Reich.* New York: Fawcett Publications, 1966.

Tuchman, Barbara W. *The Proud Tower: A Portrait of the World Before the War, 1890–1914.* New York: Bantam Books, 1967.

Waite, Robert G. L., ed. *Hitler and Nazi Germany.* New York: Holt, Rinehart and Winston, 1966.

Primary Sources and Biographies

Brecht, Bertolt. *On Theatre.* Ed. and trans. John Willett. New York: Hill and Wang, 1964.

Finck, Henry T. *Wagner and His Works.* 2 vols. New York: Scribner's, 1894.

Gauss, Christian. *The German Emperor as Shown in His Public Utterances.* New York: Scribner's, 1915.

Hitler, Adolf. *Mein Kampf.* Trans. John Chamberlain et *al.* New York: Reynal & Hitchcock, 1939.

James, Henry. *The Portable Henry James.* Ed. Morton Zabel. New York: Viking Press, 1965.

Manvell, Roger and Heinrich Fraenkel. *Dr. Goebbels: His Life and Death.* New York: Simon and Schuster, 1960.

Moeller van den Bruck, Artur. *Germany's Third Empire.* Ed. and trans. E. O. Lorimer. London: George Allen & Unwin Ltd., 1934.

Mosse, George L., ed. *Nazi Culture.* New York: Grosset & Dunlap, 1966.

Pirandello, Luigi. *Naked Masks.* Ed. Eric Bentley. New York: E. P. Dutton & Company, Inc., 1952.

Richter, Hans. *Dada: Art and Anti-Art.* New York: McGraw-Hill, 1966.

Von Bismarck, Otto. *The Kaiser vs. Bismarck.* Trans. Bernard Miall. New York: Harper & Brothers, 1921.

———. *Reflections and Reminiscences.* Ed. Theodore S. Hamerow. New York: Harper & Row, 1968.

Wagner, Richard. *Authentic Libretti of the Wagner Operas.* New York: Crown Publishers, 1938. Copyright © 1938, 1966.

Wagner, Richard. *Poems: The Ring of the Nibelung.* Rev. ed. Trans. and ed. George T. Dippold. New York: Henry Holt and Company, 1888.

William II of Germany. *The Kaiser's Speeches.* Trans. and ed. Wolf von Schierbrand. New York: Harper and Brothers, 1903.

Psychological and Sociological Studies Concerned At Least in Part with Germany

Arendt, Hannah. *Eichmann in Jerusalem: A Report on the Banality of Evil.* Rev. ed. New York: Viking Press, 1964.

———. *The Origins of Totalitarianism.* New York: Meridian Books, 1960.

Bettelheim, Bruno. *The Informed Heart: Autonomy in a Mass Age.* New York: The Free Press, 1963.

Bramsted, Ernest K. *Aristocracy and the Middle-Classes in Germany: Social Types in German Literature, 1830–1900.* Rev. ed. Chicago: University of Chicago Press, 1964.

Ellul, Jacques. *Propaganda.* Trans. Konrad Kellen and Jean Lerner. New York: Alfred A. Knopf, 1965.

Erikson, Erik H. *Childhood and Society.* 2nd ed. New York: W. W. Norton, 1963.

Frankl, Viktor E. *Man's Search for Meaning: An Introduction to Logotherapy.* New York: Washington Square Press, Inc., 1963.

Fromm, Erich. *Escape from Freedom.* New York: Avon Books, 1965.

Hoffer, Eric. *The True Believer.* New York: Harper & Row, 1966.

Koestler, Arthur. *The Yogi and the Commissar and Other Essays.* New York: Macmillan, 1967.

Kracauer, Siegfried. *From Caligari to Hitler: A Psychological History of the German Film.* Princeton, N.J.: Princeton University Press, 1947.

Methodology and Related Aesthetic and Psychological Theory

Auerbach, Erich. *Mimesis.* Trans. Willard Trask. Garden City, N.Y.: Doubleday, 1957.

Barthes, Roland. *Elements of Semiology.* Trans. Annette Lavers and Colin Smith. London: Jonathan Cape, 1967.

———. *Writing Degree Zero.* Trans. Annette Lavers and Colin Smith. London: Jonathan Cape, 1967.

Berger, Peter L. and Thomas Luckman. *The Social Construction of Reality.* Garden City, N.Y.: Doubleday, 1966.

Brown, Norman O. *Life Against Death: The Psychoanalytical Meaning of History.* New York: Random House, 1959.

Burke, Kenneth. *Attitudes Toward History.* Rev. ed. Boston: Beacon Press, 1961.

———. *A Grammar of Motives and a Rhetoric of Motives.* Berkeley, Cal.: University of California Press, 1969.

———. *Permanence and Change.* New York: New Republic, Inc., 1936.

———. *The Philosophy of Literary Form: Studies in Symbolic Action.* Rev. ed. New York: Vintage Books, 1961.

Carpenter, Edmund and Marshall McLuhan, eds. *Explorations in Communication: An Anthology.* Boston: Beacon Press, 1966.

Cassirer, Ernst. *An Essay on Man.* New Haven: Yale University Press, 1948.

—————. *The Myth of the State.* New Haven: Yale University Press, 1946.

—————. *The Philosophy of Symbolic Forms.* 3 vols. Trans. Ralph Manheim. New Haven: Yale University Press, 1953–1957.

Dean, Leonard F. "*Richard II:* The State and the Image of the Theater." *Publications of the Modern Language Association,* 67 (1952), 211–18.

De Jouvenel, Bertrand. *On Power.* Trans. J. F. Huntington. Boston: Beacon Press, 1962.

Duncan, Hugh Dalziel. *Communication and Social Order.* New York: Bedminster Press, 1962.

—————. *Culture and Democracy: The Struggle for Form in Society and Architecture in Chicago and the Middle West During the Life and Times of Louis H. Sullivan.* New York: Bedminster Press, 1965.

Edelman, Murray. *The Symbolic Uses of Politics.* Urbana, Ill.: University of Illinois Press, 1967.

Fergusson, Francis. *The Idea of a Theater.* Garden City, N.Y.: Doubleday, 1949.

Freud, Sigmund. *Civilization and Its Discontents.* Ed. and trans. James Strachey. New York: W. W. Norton, 1962.

Frye, Northrop. *Anatomy of Criticism.* Princeton, N.J.: Princeton University Press, 1957.

—————. *The Educated Imagination.* Bloomington, Ind.: Indiana University Press, 1964.

Goffman, Erving. *The Presentation of Self in Everyday Life.* Garden City, N.Y.: Doubleday, 1959.

Gusfield, Joseph R. *Symbolic Crusade.* Urbana, Ill.: University of Illinois Press, 1966.

Hall, Edward T. *The Silent Language.* New York: Fawcett Publications, 1965.

Jaspers, Karl. *Truth and Symbol.* Trans. Jean T. Wilde, William Kluback, and William Kimmel. New Haven: College and University Press, 1959.

Kenner, Hugh. *The Counterfeiters.* Bloomington, Ind.: Indiana University Press, 1968.

Kockelmans, Joseph J., ed. *Phenomenology: The Philosophy of Edmund Husserl and Its Interpretation.* Garden City, N.Y.: Doubleday, 1967.

Laing, R. D. *The Divided Self: An Existential Study in Sanity and Madness.* Baltimore: Penguin Books, 1966.

Langer, Susanne K. *Philosophy in a New Key: A Study in the Symbolism of Reason, Rite and Art.* New York: New American Library, 1951.

Lévi-Strauss, Claude. *The Scope of Anthropology.* Trans. Sherry O. and Robert A. Paul. London: Jonathan Cape, 1967.

McLuhan, Marshall. *The Gutenberg Galaxy.* Toronto: University of Toronto Press, 1965.

—————. *The Mechanical Bride.* Boston: Beacon Press, 1964.

—————. *Understanding Media.* New York: New American Library, 1966.

Mailer, Norman. *The Presidential Papers.* New York: Putnam's, 1963.

Manis, Jerome G. and Bernard N. Meltzer, eds. *Symbolic Interaction: A Reader in Social Psychology.* Boston: Allyn and Bacon, 1967.

Marcuse, Herbert. *One Dimensional Man.* Boston: Beacon Press, 1964.

Maurois, André. *Dickens.* Trans. Hamish Miles. New York: Harper & Brothers, 1935.

Mead, George H. *Mind, Self and Society.* Chicago: University of Chicago Press, 1934.

O'Brien, Conor Cruise. "Politics as Drama as Politics." *New American Review,* 4 (1968), 49–64.

Ortega y Gasset, José. *The Modern Theme.* Trans. James Cleugh. New York: Harper & Row, 1961.

Ruesch, Jurgen and Gregory Bateson. *Communication, the Social Matrix of Psychiatry.* 1st ed. New York: W. W. Norton, 1951.

Ruesch, Jurgen and Weldon Kees. *Nonverbal Communication: Notes on the Visual Perception of Human Relations.* Berkeley, Cal.: University of California Press, 1956.

Sontag, Susan. *Against Interpretation.* New York: Farrar, Straus and Giroux, 1966.

Strauss, Anselm L. *Mirrors and Masks: The Search for Identity.* Glencoe, Ill.: The Free Press, 1959.

Structuralism. Yale French Studies, 36–37 (October, 1966).

Wilson, Edmund. *To the Finland Station: A Study in the Writing and Acting of History.* Garden City, N.Y.: Doubleday 1940.

70 71 72 73   12 11 10 9 8 7 6 5 4 3 2 1